CW00531433

John Cage

Titles in the series Critical Lives present the work of leading cultural figures of the modern period. Each book explores the life of the artist, writer, philosopher or architect in question and relates it to their major works.

John Cage

Rob Haskins

REAKTION BOOKS

For Laura Kuhn, and in memoriam Merce Cunningham

Published by Reaktion Books Ltd
33 Great Sutton Street
London EC1V 0DX, UK
www.reaktionbooks.co.uk

First published 2012

Copyright © Rob Haskins 2012

All rights reserved
No part of this publication may be reproduced, stored in a retrieval system, or
transmitted, in any form or by any means, electronic, mechanical, photocopy-
ing, recording or otherwise, without the prior permission of the publishers.

Printed and bound in Great Britain
by CPI Group (UK) Ltd, Croydon, CR0 4YY

British Library Cataloguing in Publication Data
Haskins, Rob, 1960–
    John Cage. -- (Critical lives)
    1. Cage, John 2. Composers – United States -- Biography.
    I. Title II. Series
    780.9'2-DC23
    ISBN 978 1 86189 905 7

Contents

John Cage, portrait for his appointment as Charles Eliot Norton Professor of Poetry, Harvard University, 1988.

Introduction

In September 2002 one of the most bizarre legal battles regarding musical copyright was settled quietly, out of court. The music publisher C. F. Peters Corporation claimed that the English composer and producer Mike Batt had plagiarized music by John Cage (1912–1992) on an album called *Classical Graffiti*. Batt avoided the suit by donating an undisclosed sum, rumoured to be six figures, to Cage's publisher. The work in question? *4'33"* (1952), a work that requests its performer to make no sound whatsoever for any length of time.[1]

4'33", Cage's best-known composition, contains no sounds imagined by him, but rather only the sounds that naturally occur whenever and wherever the piece is performed: creaking chairs, coughs, whispers, wind (or perhaps heating or air conditioning) . . . sometimes angry outbursts. For many people became extremely angry when what Cage called 'my silent piece' was first performed. Some who hear about it for the first time respond as if he only intended the piece as a kind of flamboyant joke, Dadaist or conceptual art extended ad absurdum. Others – many others – have written at length to explore its various possible meanings.[2]

Cage's earlier career as a composer gave little indication of the extremes he would explore with *4'33"* and much of his later music. He pioneered music for percussion while a young man. In an age in which rhythm sometimes seems to have eclipsed every other element of music in importance, Cage's love for the medium – his flair for laying down a fantastic groove – still rings true in today's global musical world. He also maintained a keen interest in electronic music and in new, unusual instruments, of which the most famous is the so-called prepared piano, a grand piano with bolts, screws, rubber wedges and other materials inserted around and between the strings.

Dismayed by critics who could not apprehend the emotions he was trying to evoke in his compositions, he became convinced that self-expression represented an inadequate justification for creating music. Through the study of Indian philosophy and aesthetics in the mid-1940s, he discovered another, by way of a woman named Gita Sarabhai: 'To sober and quiet the mind and thus make it susceptible to divine influences.'[3] A few years later he became devoted to Zen Buddhism, which espoused a compassionate and non-judgemental acceptance of life as the source of sudden enlightenment.

At the beginning of the 1950s Cage's developing ideas about music and the function of the composer in society led him to work towards removing his own likes and dislikes from the act of composition so that sounds might be loved simply for what they are, rather than for how they might be used to express the personality of a composer or demonstrate his intellectual ingenuity. Using what he called 'chance operations', Cage established a new way of making compositions. He explained that his activity had changed from making choices to asking questions; he said that anyone could do what he was doing if they decided to; and he remained absolutely certain that the results of his music would open people to the possibility of enjoying sound on its own and of appreciating everyday life in its complexity, unpredictability and benign, unassuming beauty.

He was not altogether correct. Chance and indeterminate music, as Cage called it, continued to involve a great deal of his sensibility and aesthetic instincts; the considerable intricacy and time-consuming nature of composing through chance operations prevented most people from doing it as well as he; and the music occasioned a multiplicity of responses, many of which he could not sympathize with or indeed foresee.

For a long time – much too long – one of the typical responses to Cage's work reconfigured him as a sublime philosopher: a man whose path-breaking theories about art exerted an immense influence on art and artists of every possible persuasion, but whose own art never measured up to his ideas. Now, fortunately, many writers have clarified Cage's methods, and many musicians, presenters and record companies have produced first-rate performances of his compositions – both before and after his embrace of chance – that make the best possible case for their success as music.[4]

Cage himself adopted many guises throughout his lifetime: revivalist preacher for the avant-garde, gourmet cook, social commentator, mushroom expert. In addition to an extremely large catalogue of musical compositions, he also produced bodies of distinctive visual art and literature, much of which he made with the assistance of chance operations. Paradoxically, each work he made possessed an inimitable character that revealed the unmistakable identity of its maker. Consider, for instance, the excerpt shown overleaf from one of his late text compositions, the sources for which include extensive borrowing from other authors.

Or take the example of *10 Stones*, an edition of 20 aquatints printed by Marcia Bartholme on smoked paper from 1989; it was made at Crown Point Press, where Cage created the bulk of his visual art. He created the circular shapes by tracing stones with brushes; the placement of the tracings was determined by chance operations, along with the choice of colours and the number of stones traced. But the harmonization of the colours and the beautiful compositional balance between tracings and the inchoate patterns of the smoked paper are as evocative as any art created through intention alone. Taken as a whole, Cage's creative work represents a most remarkable contribution to twentieth-century art in its evocation of the wide expressive range during that turbulent period.

equally loud and in the same temPo

criticizEd south

leadeR

south aFrica's

bits Of a piece of music to have

duRing the reading

a direction Might not

thAt

the readiNg about that you would just have to say you

like this the first time and like this the seCond without

any influEnce '

equally loud and in the same temPo only

what is thE

it' well Read or

not oF the greatest

which sOmeone

impoRtance but isn't understanding shewn e.g. in

a coMposer

to progrAmme music

as loNg as

taken differently **eaCh**

playEd

equally loud and in the same temPo only

wEll

thRough experience it can never renew'[5]

    Just as Cage assumed a wide variety of stances and worked in a variety of media throughout his career, critical and creative responses to his oeuvre have engendered many different John Cages, many conflicting assessments of his project and many varied approaches to the vital creativity he practised. He has been depicted as a humourless mad scientist in the laboratory of so-called high modernism; as a groundbreaking artist who has extended the experience of art by altering the standard assumptions separating artist from audience and art from nature; and as an avuncular guru whose ideas helped foment changing aesthetics that led to the sample-laden bricolage of popular electronic music.[6]

This book presents a brief but critical introduction to Cage's life and creative work. Accordingly, not every event in his life has been described, and many of his more than 300 compositions are not mentioned. The account draws extensively on some of the important critical scholarship that has appeared in the past twenty years. Many of these sources originally appeared in professional journals or in other specialist collections not readily available and largely intended for an audience already very familiar with the abundant secondary literature. Nevertheless, the best of these sources have made great strides in demystifying John Cage's music, art and beliefs. To give only three of the many outstanding examples: Leta E. Miller has shown the degree to which Cage's Seattle colleagues and environment influenced his work; David Patterson has carefully

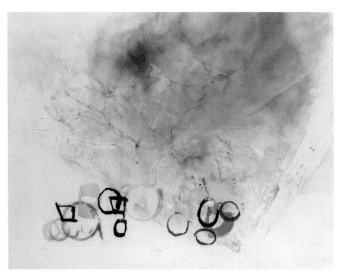

John Cage, *10 Stones*, 1989, aquatint on smoked paper in an edition of 20 (46 x 59 cm), printed by Marcia Bartholme at Crown Point Press.

traced the multilayered process through which Cage appropriated the ideas of others and reconfigured them for his own aesthetic purposes; and James Pritchett thoroughly and brilliantly explained exactly how Cage used chance operations to compose.[7] Because Cage's career was so controversial – and because he continues to inspire, amuse and confound many people of widely varying backgrounds and avocations – some demystification can only help to enrich a sense of the man.

Cage experienced no difficulties as an autobiographer. His own writings, scattered throughout a number of books and other occasional publications over the years, furnish ample material for an account in his own words. Although Cage was an unreliable historian, his own words remain as fresh and entertaining as ever; the selection I have made for this book gives a sense of the many changes of emphasis and outlook that he experienced. In a way his words function as a kind of dissonant counterpoint with the more rigorously researched history reported in the book: neither history nor memoir, but rather a particular mode of literature that falls in the margins between them.

Finally I have tried, insofar as possible, to describe not only what art, music and literature Cage made – and *how* he made it – but also how I experience it. My own memories as both a performer and as an audience member for concerts of Cage's music have shaped my feelings about his work in countless ways. In 1992, shortly after Cage's death, I began rehearsing *Two²* (1989) for a concert with Laurel Karlik Sheehan, the pianist who had given the work's Canadian premiere with Jack Behrens. As the rehearsals proceeded, I was struck by the beauty of the chords in the piece, and later shocked when so many of them recurred three and sometimes four times. (I had always thought that chance music had no patterns whatsoever.)

Later I attended the premiere of the solo violin piece *One¹⁰* (1992) at Goucher College on 4 April 1993. Cage made this unusual work to accompany an engaging sculpture installation by Mineko Grimmer, an inverted pyramid of ice that she encrusted with pebbles and suspended from the roof of the space; she also placed a pool of water on the floor and a copper wire between pool and sculpture. As the ice melted, the pebbles fell into the pool. Sometimes the pebbles struck the wire, producing a short sound; but sometimes they missed the wire entirely and I heard only the noise the pebbles made when they struck the water.

As the violin music – which consisted solely of harmonics sustained for long periods – continued over the work's 24-minute duration, an unusual effect set in quite unlike any Western classical music I have ever heard. My mind became still, barely on the edge of consciousness. The opportunity to experience the span of time as a dynamic entity disappeared and I could no longer perceive the passing minutes. *One¹⁰*'s premiere offered the possibility to enter an alternative state of consciousness that stands outside ordinary modes of perception.

In short, I am unabashedly and intensely moved by Cage's music both before and after his turn to chance, although I confess that I cannot always describe the feelings that it evokes for me. I believe, however, that it reaffirms my conviction that a perennial dialogue between the unfamiliar and the conventional is immanent to artistic experience. For this reason, perhaps more than any other, I hope this book will generate a greater interest in the sound of Cage's music – even as it acknowledges his considerable achievement in literature and visual art – and furthermore that this awareness helps to change the impression that our time is one of unrelieved irony and scepticism.

1

Becoming

The year 1912 was an auspicious one in the history of European classical music. Claude Debussy completed a ballet, *Jeux*, to be premiered the next year by Diaghilev's Ballets Russes; Debussy had almost single-handedly re-established Paris as an important site for new music. Igor Stravinsky, a Russian also working in Paris, had electrified Parisian art circles with his own works for the Ballets Russes, *The Firebird* and *Petrushka*; he was now composing a third ballet, *The Rite of Spring*, whose visceral rhythms, dissonant harmonies and disjunct form would soon establish him as one of the pre-eminent modernist composers. In Berlin, Arnold Schoenberg led the premiere of his Expressionist masterpiece, *Pierrot Lunaire* – the odd combination of cabaret and wiry, dissonant polyphony resonated with its large and appreciative first audience, and the piece went on to successful European tours.

In the USA, by contrast, nineteenth-century European traditions continued to dominate musical life. Many professional American composers had actually completed their training in Germany under such composers as Joseph Rheinberger or Hans Pfitzner, and they returned to perpetuate the musical forms and modes of expression they had learned there. Some, such as Arthur Farwell, leavened their training abroad with the sounds and affect of Native American culture. Farwell set these works first in European style, and later in more austere harmonies and rhythms that stressed their distance from the European tradition. Even so, he and his fellow 'Indianists' cultivated a parasitic and exploitative relationship with Native American culture in spite of their good intentions; such exoticism was ultimately unsustainable. And although Charles Ives, the greatest American composer of the early twentieth century, composed the bulk of his music during the first two decades of the century, he was largely unknown, spending his days working in the insurance industry and writing music in his free time. His work would not reach a large public until the late 1920s and '30s.

If the so-called art music of America remained largely in Europe's shadow, the country itself made tremendous strides forward during the first decade of the twentieth century. The Progressive Era witnessed the US's assertion of itself as an influential world power. America began to confront a host of social ills including the working conditions of women and children, a 'living wage' and voting rights for women. It was a time in which experts turned their attention to optimizing industry. Fordism made manufactured goods available to factory workers just as surely as it transformed those workers into disenfranchised cogs who functioned separately and anonymously in a massive structure of flesh, blood, sinew and bone. Taylorism created a benign network of middle-level managers who alienated those beneath them and were themselves alienated by managers above them. These methods were increasingly applied to government as well. All this made America a better functioning, more prosperous country but left many people feeling somehow less than human. Only the onset of the First World War and America's somewhat belated decision to enter it allowed the country to forge a sense of societal unity fuelled by fundamental beliefs in morality and democracy.

The state of California, John Cage's home, was shaped by this momentous time but also influenced by conditions quite different from the centres of American politics and power on the opposite coast, some 3,000 miles distant. Its large size – nearly twice that of Great Britain – helped to ensure a heterogeneous population made

John Milton Cage,
late 1930s or 1940s.

still more diverse by a large number of immigrants, particularly Asians, whose presence created further cultural tensions. In the south, the state's proximity to Mexico and the many Spanish-speaking people living in California raised awareness of the social injustices of the Diáz regime preceding the Mexican Revolution; several prominent Mexican revolutionaries were active in Los Angeles during the 1910s and were supported by socialists and anarchists. California as a whole suffered from political corruption and a protracted struggle between pro- and anti-union interests.[1] In such an environment, individual voices seemed to have little agency and no one course of action presented itself as the right one.

It was into this paradoxical situation that Cage was born on 5 September 1912 in the southern California city of Los Angeles, which at the time was beginning to rival San Francisco's prestige and influence.[2] And that state of paradox extended even to Cage's parents and forebears. His father, John Milton Cage, worked as a freelance inventor; cheerful, somewhat wandering in spirit, and a little absent-minded, Cage *père* combined an inventor's questing spirit with a certain distrust for intellectual display. (He once wrote a paper to argue that Einstein's theories could be expressed far more simply than the way Einstein had himself formulated them.[3]) Cage's paternal grandfather, a minister who founded the first Methodist Episcopal church in Denver, regarded John Milton as the black sheep of the family.

Cage's mother, Lucretia Harvey Cage ('Crete'), was an enigma all on her own. A very independent-minded woman, she frequently found herself utterly exasperated by her husband's casual approach to life. However, a certain Bohemianism in her own nature (she had been married twice previously) was tempered by a family background of strong Protestant faith; the severity of religious conviction would

Lucretia ('Crete')
Harvey Cage, *c.* 1925.

be passed along to her son. Crete's various occupations included editing the women's club column for the anti-union *Los Angeles Times*; she was part of a nationwide group of women that took leading roles in shaping both small- and large-scale cultural institutions of all sorts in America.[4]

With the exception of a four-year period in Michigan and Ontario, where the family lived while John Milton Cage worked in Ann Arbor for the war effort, the boy's formative experiences occurred in California. Their residence served as home to an extended family comprising Crete's relations, including her mother, sister and brother-in-law. The grandmother, whom Cage had dubbed Minnehaha owing to her jet-black hair, made a particularly strong impression on the child. She held particularly strong Christian beliefs and regularly had him join her for responsive Bible readings. Once, he crept into the room to retrieve a manuscript while she slept; snoring as a radio sermon played full blast in the room, she suddenly awoke and demanded, 'John, are you ready for the second coming of the Lord?'[5]

Such stringent reinforcement of fundamental Christian beliefs often leaves young children with a heightened sense of morality and an extremely serious approach to everyday life, one markedly different from their peers. Young John felt a keen sense of otherness from this and other factors. He was a precocious child, graduating from high school at the age of fifteen. Early photographs suggest that he was an overly beautiful boy, gentle with animals, perhaps a bit effeminate. Certainly others thought so, too: he was mercilessly bullied as a child; the children laughed at him, called him a sissy, even physically assaulted him. The lonely child, who believed in pacifism and strongly responded to the significant influence of his Christian relations, would literally turn the other cheek to his attackers.[6]

Cage responded to harassment and loneliness by turning inward. Without a large group of peers and friends to help guide his

John Cage, *c.* 1918.

development, he discovered himself through solitary pursuits. He recalled being sent to the beach every day as a child, where he rolled a rubber ball through complicated tracks of his own design, but he never mentioned a friend who joined him.[7] He also read a great deal and soon found solace in music. Many American families still owned pianos in the early years of the twentieth century; Cage began to play in 1920, crediting Phoebe James, his maternal aunt, as his principal teacher. Because Aunt Phoebe's tastes tended towards bourgeois nineteenth-century salon music, she discouraged the young boy from such serious composers as Bach and Beethoven and favoured instead Romantic composers like Moszkowski and Grieg; their modest works were frequently published in anthologies designed for mass consumption with such good-natured titles as *Music the Whole World Loves to Play*.[8]

Ambitious young children who learn the piano work assiduously to master it by practising scales, arpeggios and other technical studies in addition to perfecting solo pieces for their recitals; Cage's aspirations were quite different. With Aunt Phoebe's help, he refined the skill of sight reading, moving quickly from one new piece to another without necessarily feeling obligated to learn any single work thoroughly. In this fashion, the boy had a ready supply of new experiences, new discoveries – enough to amuse and comfort him.

Cage's proficiency with the piano gave him poise and confidence; he began to turn outward. Auditioning for the high school glee club, he was told he did not have a voice. Later, for the radio station KNX, he offered his services as producer and host of a weekly broadcast designed to present the talents of his fellow boy scouts (Cage never progressed to the highest level of Eagle Scout himself); acting as master of ceremonies, he introduced his peers who performed instrumental solos that he accompanied on the piano. The show's two-year run also included adult speakers who offered short, inspirational homilies and, when all else failed, piano solos from the host himself.[9]

But music was not Cage's sole passion during these years. His own interests in spirituality led him away from the rather ascetic practices of his Protestant background towards the much more flamboyant practices of the Liberal Catholic Church, whose rituals struck him as a medley of the most theatrical elements from countless faiths; he even considered choosing the church over his own parents until a priest told him, 'Don't be a fool. Go home. There are many religions. You have only one mother and father.'[10] He also excelled at languages, studying French and Greek in high school as well as English composition and literature.

In May 1927 he successfully competed in a regional oratorical contest, presenting his winning entry, 'Other People Think', at the Hollywood Bowl. This speech gave unmistakable evidence of Cage's particular background in the California of the early twentieth century as well as a glimpse of the artist and thinker he would become. In it he criticized the American 'capitalists who have zealously invested money in the Southern Republics and eagerly exploited them'.[11] His solution to this social problem did not require political action, but rather, an astonishing vision of nationwide paralysis:

> One of the greatest blessings that the United States could receive in the near future would be to have her industries halted, her business discontinued, her people speechless, a great pause in her world of affairs created, and finally to have everything stopped that runs, until everyone should hear the last wheel go around and the last echo fade away . . . then, in that moment of complete intermission, of undisturbed calm, would be the hour most conducive to the birth of a Pan-American Conscience . . . For we should be hushed and silent, and we should have the opportunity to learn that other people think.[12]

Cage hoped that both the us and its Latin American neighbours could learn to understand their separate differences of cultural attitude and so value each other more than they ever had before. He was only fourteen when he delivered these extraordinary words. One year later he graduated from Los Angeles High School as the valedictorian of his class.

After high school, Cage matriculated at Pomona College. He soon bristled at the idea of organized education, wondering, for instance, why everyone had to read the same book instead of reading different books and sharing their newly acquired knowledge with one another. For assignments and tests, he wrote responses in the manner of modern literature, emulating Gertrude Stein; this creative approach earned him an A the first time he tried it and a failing mark thereafter. His musical interests widened to include Beethoven's string quartets, which he listened to with Tamio Abe, a Japanese friend who owned 'as fine a collection of those as one could find'.[13]

Two years later, Cage left Pomona without earning a degree. After hitchhiking from California to Texas, he boarded a ship bound for Le Havre. He had decided that he wanted to pursue a career as a writer, and convinced his parents to support him financially while he gathered life experiences and self-education abroad. But his recollections of that time contain little detail on any prose or poetry he made. Instead, Cage seemed at first to have spent most of his time with art. In the Bibliothèque Mazarine, he studied Gothic architecture from the time the library opened until it closed. An art historian whom Cage had met while at Pomona, José Pijoán, happened upon him and, learning what Cage was doing, gave him a 'kick in the pants' and helped introduce him to a more modern architect, Ernö Goldfinger. Under Goldfinger's direction, Cage set to work drawing Greek columns and measuring apartments that the architect had been hired to renovate. One day, when he overheard Goldfinger telling a group of female admirers that an architect had to devote his life to architecture, Cage tendered his resignation, stating as his reason that he could not devote his life to architecture. It is just as likely that he was equally offended by Goldfinger's attitude: the serious young man probably did not imagine that modern art included making time to dally with young women.[14]

Apparently unable to decide between music, art and literature, Cage now explored all three freely. He took a few lessons at the Paris Conservatoire with Lazare-Lévy, a famed French pianist and pedagogue who championed new music and whose many students included Solomon, Monique Haas, Clara Haskil and Yvonne Loriod. His musical tastes expanded to include Bach and Mozart, and a fortuitous piano recital by John Kirkpatrick (who would premiere Charles Ives's 'Concord' Sonata in 1939) included works by Skryabin and Stravinsky, whetting Cage's appetite for new music. Soon thereafter Cage encountered *Das Neue Klavierbuch* (issued by the German publisher B. Schott's Söhne), an anthology of easy piano pieces by modern composers including Stravinsky, Bartók and Hindemith.

But perhaps Cage's most important discovery came in 1931: a deep romantic relationship with Don Sample, a poet who had studied at

Harvard. He was not the first of Cage's male partners; nor was Cage attracted exclusively to men, either before or after their time together. But Sample's role in his life was significant, and their relationship was perhaps the first important one in Cage's life: they remained together for several years, even living together in California after their European sojourn. Sample, described by a mutual acquaintance as 'an egotistical and exacting Harvard type',[15] helped to shape Cage's interests in art and introduced him to the avant-garde literary periodical *transition*; there, Cage read fragments from a work in progress by James Joyce that would become *Finnegans Wake*, a book that came to hold the highest importance for Cage's own work.

The couple's travels exposed them to some of the most influential art of the time. In Majorca the two men had occasional interactions with Robert Graves. There, too, Cage began composing music in earnest; most of the works, which he described as created with the aid of mathematical calculations and all of very short duration, still exist despite his later claims that he destroyed them.[16] In Dessau the couple also visited the Bauhaus and were impressed with its modernist aesthetic of combining fine art and industrial design, technology and precise measurement.[17] Although Cage invariably recalled the influence of such visual artists as László Moholy-Nagy and Josef Albers, Oskar Schlemmer's concept of the theatre as spatial art – where every sector of the space, every possible movement of an actor within that space, should be considered as a potential site for action – suggests very strong affinities to Cage's own later work with dance and theatre.[18]

When Cage had felt, early in his European travels, a pang of homesickness, his parents urged him to stay on. 'Don't be a fool', Crete chided; 'Stay in Europe as long as possible. . . . You'll probably never get there again.'[19] Eventually, however, the financial pressures of the Great Depression prevented his parents from continuing their financial support. He and Sample travelled back to America, driving cross-country in a Ford Model T for the final leg of their journey. By 1932 they were living together in Santa Monica, a city surrounded on three sides by Los Angeles.

They lived together in an apartment with a large room above an auto court; Cage did the gardening in exchange for rent. With very little money available, he did not have the luxury to concentrate on any one artistic activity to the exclusion of all else. Perhaps he also felt that his own cultural education was as yet incomplete, for he soon began earning income as a freelance educator, presenting weekly lectures on modern art and music to women in the neigh-bourhood. In France he had already done occasional work as a tour guide for Versailles and other similar sites. Not knowing anything about them beforehand, he learned everything he could the day before the presentations; he once confessed this modus operandi to a group of people, who responded that they were already aware of his naivety and all the more entertained by it.[20] No doubt the California housewives were equally charmed by his infectious enthusiasm for the subjects he spoke about and by the feeling that they were learning much at the same time as he.

Along the way, Cage made some opportunities to present his own music. With Harry Hay, best known today as an important gay rights activist and founder of the Mattachine Society support group, he pre-sented some of his early songs for the Santa Monica Women's Club in November 1932. In this most recent music, Cage had abandoned his previous method of composing with complex mathematics and now pursued a kind of notated improvisation in which he wrote down what he spontaneously created at the piano as quickly as possible.

Crete may have used her connections to help produce the concert; early in his career, she would be fond of overstating the extent of his musical training, particularly his studies with Lazare-Lévy. With Cage at the piano, Hay presented the songs in the quasi-geometric costumes and objective performance style associated with the theatrical aesthetic of the Bauhaus. (The singer recalled that he, Cage and Sample frequently studied Bauhaus catalogues that the couple brought back with them from Europe for ideas about furniture and design.[21])

Cage's lectures for housewives, meanwhile, proceeded without incident until he began preparing one on Schoenberg. Recordings were scarce. Nor was performance an option: the composer's piano music poses notorious technical challenges to musicians, and Cage's modest skills prevented him from playing almost all of it. On an earlier occasion, he correctly and incredibly guessed that the American pianist Richard Buhlig, who had performed Schoenberg's Three Piano Pieces (Op. 11), was now living in Los Angeles. With characteristic confidence, he telephoned Buhlig and asked for a private performance of the Op. 11 pieces, but the pianist refused and hung up abruptly. Now he thought again of Buhlig as a possible resource for his Schoenberg lecture:

> I decided not to telephone him but to go directly to his house and visit him. I hitchhiked into Los Angeles, arriving at his house at noon. He wasn't home. I took a pepper bough off a tree and, pulling off the leaves one by one, recited, 'He'll come home; he won't; he'll come home . . .' It always turned out He'll come home. He did. At midnight.[22]

Although Buhlig refused to help him, he was impressed enough to make another appointment with the younger man to take a look at his compositions.

This meeting proved very providential, because thereafter Buhlig helped to refine Cage's compositional skills. While the pianist always stopped short of describing his advice as compositional instruction, his substantial performance repertoire of twentieth-century music no doubt gave him considerable insights into any new music. He admonished his student to read basic writings on musical harmony and form by the nineteenth-century English composer Ebenezer

Prout and to abandon improvisation in favour of some sort of coherent compositional design; Cage turned away from improvisation and song towards creating instrumental music with strict, abstract titles like 'sonata', 'composition' and 'pieces'.

The *Sonata for Clarinet* (1933), arguably Cage's first important early piece written under Buhlig's supervision, nevertheless suggests very little to distinguish it as music written by a composer of great promise. Cast in the familiar form of three movements – the outer two fast and the inner, slow – it lasts only three minutes. The clarinet line twists and undulates around all twelve pitches of the chromatic scale, and frequent leaps to the instrument's extreme registers only reinforce the impression of disarray. But some melodic and rhythmic patterns occasionally return to guide the listener; elsewhere, two melodies reappear in reverse order from their original statements. (In fact, the final movement repeats all the pitch material from the first movement in this fashion.[23])

Grete Sultan, *c.* 1950.

What gives the piece its memorable character, however, derives from Cage's handling of rhythm and instinct for pacing and compelling musical closure. Within the apparent confusion of the first movement, he builds a frantic sense of forward momentum by interrupting a steady stream of short notes with sudden arabesques and longer tones. Each group of steady notes varies in number, obscuring a sense of regular metre but increasing the excitement of the music's flow. He also effects a dramatic and satisfying ending by a sudden slowing to longer note values that is made even more emphatic by the wide leaps in register. Cage was justly proud of his sonata.

Buhlig also helped to foster his connections to other musicians in the area. He introduced him to other students, one of whom – Grete Sultan – would become a lifelong friend and advocate for his music. Perhaps most important, Buhlig encouraged him to submit the newly finished clarinet sonata to the American composer Henry Cowell for possible publication in Cowell's quarterly periodical devoted to contemporary composition, *New Music*.

Cowell, whose music Buhlig had championed since the 1920s, was the most famous American composer living on the West Coast and perhaps the most important American modernist composer known at the time. He had overcome considerable social and economic disadvantage through a combination of perseverance, voracious curiosity and a singular personality that announced itself to several people, including the musicologist and composer Charles Seeger, who were able to help him complete his education. Cowell was responsible for a number of innovations that had considerable influence on other composers, including tone clusters, simultaneous streams of music unfolding in different tempos, alterations to the piano for the purpose of exploiting new sonic resources and even an original idea called 'elastic form', which permitted some flexibility in a composition's formal design. Bartók and Schoenberg both respected his work, and Cowell theorized these and many other ideas in his *New Musical Resources*, a book that he began writing as early as 1916.[24]

Cowell declined to publish the clarinet sonata, but he did promise to programme it on one of his new music concerts in San Francisco. After hitchhiking there to hear the performance, Cage was mortified to learn that the clarinettist had not bothered to look at the music until the day of the concert and was now unable to cope with its formidable technical difficulties. Cage found himself obliged to play it himself on the piano in the most ridiculous way imaginable, with one finger.[25]

Notwithstanding his artistic activities, Cage seemed to be living a very precarious existence. Jobs were hard to come by and he made ends meet by doing library research for his father and helping his mother run a non-profit shop that gave area artists and craftspeople the opportunity to sell their wares. One day he experienced what he described as love at first sight when a young woman named Xenia Kashevaroff, an Alaskan native who was studying art at Reed College, came into the store. His charm and poise deserted him on their initial encounter, however; she rebuffed his offers of attention and left shortly thereafter. Nevertheless, Cage, convinced that she would return, was not dissuaded:

> Of course, in a few weeks she did. This time I had carefully prepared what I was going to say to her. That evening we had dinner and the same evening I asked her to marry me . . . She was put off a little but a year or so later, she agreed.[26]

The marriage to Xenia would hardly lead to some sort of happy ending for Cage; in fact, he would continue his relationship with Sample until 1935, even become involved both casually and seriously with other men and women. Still, Cage correctly realized that Xenia would be a very important person in his life. For a few years – until the early 1940s – their relationship would bring him a great deal of stability, happiness and inspiration.

2

Audacity

In an interview with Thomas J. Hines, conducted only a few months before his death, Cage recalled that his relationship with Don Sample had 'become promiscuous' around the time that he had proposed to Xenia. In the absence of centralized venues where gay and bisexual men could meet and openly socialize, both men cruised area parks for sex or companionship. Assuming that the couple had been completely exclusive before that time, one wonders what led them to seek other partners. Cage, who had a tendency to discuss his personal life with very little acknowledgement of those who shared that life with him, would only say that his own promiscuity owed to his inability 'to practice the emotions correctly'.[1]

This remark, and his life during the mid-1930s in general, suggests that Cage's serious commitment to creativity also manifested itself in an equally strong need for passionate interactions with people and that these connections left him feeling guilty and frequently confused. These periodic surges of passion seemed to have ceased, at least temporarily, when he finally married Xenia in an Arizona desert at 4:30 on a June morning in 1935; he ended his relationship with Sample thereafter. For the moment, however – that is, the tumultuous period in his life from the autumn of 1934 to the following spring – Cage pursued music and romance with equal vigour.

Cowell, who must have been impressed with Cage's tenacity in his one-finger piano performance of the clarinet sonata, took him on as a student. The older man could easily have recognized much of himself in the younger. Both had proved capable of learning a great deal on their own; both grew up in California; both were excited about the avant-garde in all its forms; and both had developed intimate relationships with both men and women, although no documentation exists suggesting Cage and his teacher had ever been involved with each other sexually.[2] Not much later, in 1936, Cowell would enter a tragic period in his life in which he was arrested, tried and convicted for sexual activities with younger men; his subsequent incarceration at San Quentin fortunately lasted only four years.[3] After a pardon from the governor, he lost much of his taste for extreme musical innovation; to this day his large and extremely heterogeneous output makes an assessment of his work difficult, and his considerable importance in the history of American music remains sadly underestimated.

Cowell and Cage shared one other important affinity, for the music and compositional aesthetics of Arnold Schoenberg. Forced to flee Germany because of his Jewish heritage, the composer settled first in New York and then, by the autumn of 1934, in southern California, where he taught at the University of Southern California and at the University of California at Los Angeles, as well as privately. Cowell was one of the most vocal of his supporters, publishing a laudatory assessment the previous year.[4] In the early years of the twentieth century, Cage and Cowell – along with many others – believed that modern music could only develop according to the practice of two composers: Schoenberg or Igor Stravinsky. By the 1930s, Stravinsky – ironically also living in southern California, a short distance from Schoenberg – represented the pinnacle of neo-classicism, in which the forms, harmonies, melodies and rhythms of eighteenth-century music underwent modernist transformation to return as a strong foundation for new music. Schoenberg, meanwhile, had developed the compositional approach of twelve-note music that largely abandoned the harmonic and melodic resources Stravinsky employed in order to explore the implications of uniquely ordered configurations of the chromatic scale. The sense of a tonal centre – apparent in most neo-classical music – disappeared in Schoenberg's work, replaced by new notions of coherence offered by particular orderings of the twelve chromatic pitches. Schoenberg's penchant for complex polyphony and his tendency to avoid literal musical repetition made his music sound utterly different from Stravinsky's, despite the fact that he too began to adopt eighteenth-century musical forms and gestures.

As Schoenberg criticized Stravinsky and other neo-classicists for not embracing the full ramifications of modernity and rejecting all references to tonality, so Cage decided that a commitment to the avant-garde needed to be total; he declared his allegiance to Schoenberg and to uncompromising innovation. At the time, however, very little of Schoenberg's music had been performed in America and, although scores were available for study, the exact details of Schoenberg's twelve-note music were not particularly well understood. One idea, however, united Schoenberg with a number of early twentieth-century American composers who were also attracted to his approach: a regular and systematic circulation of all twelve tones in the chromatic scale with the aim of making no one of these tones more important than any other.[5]

Cage's next pieces extended this principle in an ingenious and, as it turned out, prescient manner. He conceptualized all the pitch resources for a single piece as the twelve notes of the chromatic scale duplicated one octave above or below to produce a total of 25 pitches. Cage organized the material in these pieces in such a way that no note of the 25 could reappear until the others had occurred. This additional adjustment to the standard twelve-note universe differed a great deal from the approach of Schoenberg and others, in which the chromatic collection was treated abstractly irrespective of higher or lower register. (Similarly, musicians and their audiences are taught to think of the middle C of the piano as sharing a certain abstract identity with the cs in the next lower or higher register – as demonstrated in the familiar musical phrase, 'Do–re–mi–fa–so–la–ti–do!' from *The Sound of Music*.) Cage's method, by contrast, made him begin to think of the so-called related pitches as somehow *fundamentally* different in kind and augured his later interest in sounds divorced from a pre-existing theoretical context.

Aside from this innovation, Cage's 25-note music sounds very similar to the *Sonata for Clarinet*. The melodic lines of *Sonata for Two Voices* (1933) follow the same periphrastic path as the earlier piece, the rhythms are equally unpredictable, the three individual movements just as brief. The only difference is the presence of the second 'voice'. (In contrapuntal music, whether vocal or instrumental, the separate parts are always referred to as voices, implying their melodic independence.) The combination of two melodic lines creates greater dissonance by clashing with each other as they unfold in time. In fact, the sound of the music was widely known as dissonant counterpoint (the term was coined by Cowell's teacher Charles Seeger), in which harmonious, consonant sounds were subservient to the dissonant ones (just as the reverse holds in standard sixteenth- and eighteenth-century counterpoint).

Cage's attitudes about composition were shaped by the composers that he admired and by a certain joy in the technical process of composition itself; he commented approvingly on a book he was then reading, a series of interviews and analyses edited by Cowell.[6] This did not mean, however, that Cage thought of his music as an intellectual exercise only, but that its expressive content somehow communicated itself as a result of a composer's way of life and his beliefs; he looked forward to a day when the names of individual composers would no longer matter, 'and that a period will approach by way of common belief, selflessness, and technical mastery that will be a period of Music and not of Musicians'.[7]

The somewhat ambiguous attitude towards emotions Cage expressed in this short essay – not unlike his public reticence about

Pauline Schindler, 1930s.

the people he cared for most – helps to motivate a perennial question that musicians, writers and audiences have asked about his work: does it evoke expression? If so, what kind? It is a commonplace to argue that Cage's music evokes no emotion whatsoever. But even Cage's public statements – like those above – suggest another inter-pretation: he might not have meant that the new period of music he hoped for suppressed emotion or individuality, but rather that it engendered a new form of subjectivity, yet unknown, to be discovered and shared by all humanity.

The little essay appeared in an issue (dated 15 February 1934) of the monthly periodical *Dune Forum*, whose subscriber list included Cowell, the choreographer Martha Graham, the poet Robinson Jeffers and the architect Richard Neutra. Cage apparently sent the original manuscript along with a friendly letter to the associate editor, Pauline Schindler, who had possibly met him through Cowell.[8] The two held common beliefs; Schindler was a vigorous proponent of modern music and had written enthusiastically about Edgard Varèse. To her, Cage had already dedicated his *Composition for Three Voices* (completed in January 1934), another of the severe works written according to his 25-note system.

His deepening friendship with Schindler had to be put on hold, however, because he soon embarked on another trip, this time to New York, where he would continue his studies. Cowell knew of his ambition to study with Schoenberg and his need for financial assistance to do so; in order to help him reach the required technical proficiency for this undertaking, he advised Cage to contact Adolph Weiss, a German émigré in New York who had studied with Schoenberg and was familiar with his pedagogical methods.[9] Cage and Sample departed in April, hitchhiking across the country until they reached their destination.

In New York Weiss taught Cage such basic musical skills as how to write a good melody and how that melody might be harmonized. Cage took a menial job as a wall washer for a YWCA; his parents also sent him a small amount of money every month. His schedule was arduous: the lessons with Weiss took place at night and were frequently followed by games of bridge with Weiss, his wife and the composer Wallingford Riegger. Cage rose every morning at four o'clock to complete his assignments for the day's lesson, waiting until the last possible moment to catch the bus that would take him to his job. Taking pity on him, Weiss later gave him some work copying manuscripts in ink.[10]

Cage also saw a great deal of Henry Cowell, who had been invited to the well-known artist's school, the New School for Social Research, to teach courses in modern music and world music (the latter rather extraordinary for the time). The young man acted as Cowell's assistant and also attended his courses with the help of scholarship money made available through the beneficence of Charles Ives. The studies occupied him until December, when Weiss got a job as a bassoonist in a travelling orchestra; Cowell offered to drive Cage and Sample back to California.

Cage wrote to Pauline before setting out on his journey, so excited at the prospect of seeing her again that his letter trailed off into giddy, incomprehensible effusion: 'Everything is important. Equalities distinctions writing them out and emphasizing them.'[11] By this time, Schindler lived some 70 miles away from Los Angeles in Ojai. Cage wrote to her often and presumably consummated his relationship with her during a visit sometime in January 1935. The lovers were given to poetic ramblings about both music and nature. Schindler wrote, perhaps as a reflection on their lovemaking:

> oh, perfume is utterance. and blooming is an act of love. i believe that a part of the great meaning for human beings of loving, is the sudden power it gives them knowing the earth more fully, of entering into communication with the essential forces, to which we are usually dull and asleep . . . john, john, i am glad of you.[12]

Their ecstasy was not to last. Cage continued his relationship with Sample and, by March, announced to Pauline that Xenia had accepted his marriage proposal and that they were to be married in June. Perhaps, too, Cage continued his promiscuity with other men; in another letter, he alludes to some anguished internal conflict:

> Oh, Pauline, I know what good is, and I'm not good.
>
> To be with you would be too easy now. It would be an escape from something I must meet – this muddle. I want to conquer and then come to you. You see how evil and proud I am. The only conquest is through humility and I am not humble now.[13]

Arnold Schoenberg, *c.* 1948.

During this period, Cage studied the French horn and began his studies with Schoenberg. He abandoned the horn by the summer, but his work with Schoenberg – the exact nature of which remains somewhat unclear – continued through 1937.[14] Cage joined a large class in which Schoenberg supervised analyses of Bach's *Art of Fugue* and *Well-Tempered Clavier*, the last two Brahms symphonies and his own third string quartet. As a composer Schoenberg, who was fascinated in his own music by the way that small parcels of music – often no more than three notes – could be used to create much larger works, impressed upon his students that the great composers of the German tradition thought the same way. Cage's later courses over the next two years included composition, harmony, analysis and counterpoint.

His early reports of his studies suggest his performance under Schoenberg's tutelage had a rocky start. In April, he told Weiss, 'Although in each one of the class sessions I have "gleaned" something extremely valuable, I have felt disturbed fundamentally by the mediocrity induced by the class members. Including myself, for it seems to me that I am dull at present.' But only a month later, in a letter to Pauline Schindler, he characterized Schoenberg as a kindly and supportive teacher who held Cage's counterpoint exercises up to other students as models, so superior that he never had to look at them.[15]

Between the two letters, he had a momentous private appointment with Schoenberg in early May. During that meeting Cage answered a number of questions that he thought laid bare the considerable gaps in his musical understanding; at the end of the interrogation, however, Schoenberg permitted Cage to continue his studies with him, dismissing the student with this exhortation: 'Now you must think of nothing but music: and must work from six to eight hours a day.'[16]

Throughout his life, Cage constantly cited figures of immense authority or inspiration that had significantly shaped his own life and work, often altering and intensifying details of his encounters with the icons in the process. His memories of Schoenberg, the first of these figures, convey the sense of a grand creation myth. Here, for instance, is one of his recollections of the meeting discussed above: '[Schoenberg] said, "You probably can't afford my price", and I said, "You don't need to mention it because I don't have any money." So he said, "Will you devote your life to music?" and I said I would.'[17] Cage probably meant this account less as a wilful reconstruction of the truth than as a poetic appropriation of the facts intended to bolster his own evolving sense of himself and his aesthetic. In fact, the tone of the remark resonates harmoniously with statements in his *Dune Forum* essay describing the necessity of the artist to manifest unshakable belief and to create the kind of art demonstrating how he lives. And it explains why Cage constantly characterized his attitude towards Schoenberg as one of a disciple, not a student.

Much later, the critic and entrepreneur Peter Yates would publish a poignant (and probably embellished) account of his last conversation with Schoenberg, during which the composer – who could think only of Cage – exclaimed, 'He is not a composer, but an inventor – of genius.' This story, too, Cage readily incorporated into the legend of his time with Schoenberg.[18]

Just as the teenaged Cage delighted in the mystery and ritual of the Liberal Catholic Church, he venerated the questions and paradoxes of Schoenberg's instruction. When his students completed their counterpoint exercises too strictly, he told them not to follow the rules too seriously; when they took liberties, he criticized them for disobeying the rules. Another counterpoint class led to this mystifying exchange:

> We were to solve a particular problem he had given and to turn around when finished so that he could check on the correctness of the solution. I did as directed. He said, 'That's good. Now find another solution.' I did. He said, 'Another.' Again I found one. Again he said, 'Another.' And so on. Finally, I said, 'There are no more solutions.' He said, 'What is the principle underlying all the solutions?'[19]

The question haunted him, and he would not arrive at an answer that satisfied him until much later.

Throughout his studies, Cage regarded his tenuous understanding of harmony as his greatest Achilles heel. In their May meeting,

Schoenberg told him that one of his advanced students might help him make up what he didn't know. By the autumn, however, he again faced his *bête noire* in what was probably his final course with Schoenberg. Devotion to Schoenberg had now become difficult: the pressures of newly married life took their toll on him, and new interests – particularly in the world of percussion music – became increasingly incompatible with Schoenberg's pitch-centred view of composition. Finally, master and disciple reached an impasse:

> After I had been studying with him for two years, Schoenberg said, 'In order to write music, you must have a feeling for harmony.' I explained to him that I had no feeling for harmony. He then said that I would always encounter an obstacle, that it would be as though I came to a wall through which I could not pass. I said, 'In that case I will devote my life to beating my head against that wall.'[20]

All the composers in Schoenberg's pantheon of great composers, especially Beethoven and Wagner, had made substantial contributions to the development of harmony; Schoenberg's own 'emancipation of the dissonance' led ineluctably to the most radical developments in harmony imaginable. Cage's indifference to harmony must have shaken his teacher to the core.

For his part, Cage had become increasingly aware of an area in new music composition that could not be accommodated by Schoenberg's interests in harmony: percussion. Varèse's *Ionisation*, the first major work for percussion alone, had been premiered in New York in 1933 and influenced a flowering of interest in the medium, including such works as Cowell's *Ostinato pianissimo* (1934). Cage heard a performance of *Ionisation* at the Hollywood Bowl, and his own fascination for percussion instruments had been further stimulated by a casual remark made by the abstract filmmaker Oskar Fischinger, whom Cage assisted earlier in the spring: 'He said that everything in the world has a spirit which is released by its sound, and that set me on fire, so to speak.'[21]

While living and studying bookbinding with a woman named Hazel Dreis, Cage and Xenia formed a quartet of percussionists, which began performing on their own and as part of Cage's work accompanying and writing music for modern dance classes. Now emboldened by these experiences – and perhaps hoping to gain Schoenberg's approval for his own sonic innovations – the former student invited the teacher to his concerts. Schoenberg politely declined at least one invitation and, when another was extended for a date of his own choosing, replied, 'I am not free at any time.'[22] Cage got the message.

After Cage booked a few further performances and struggled to make ends meet with a patchwork of different jobs, including some work with his Aunt Phoebe for a high school course called 'Musical Accompaniments for Rhythmic Expression', he and Xenia began a slow migration northward and spent some time in San Francisco, where they met the composer Lou Harrison. Cage continued his work composing percussion music and also began accompanying dancers at Mills College in Oakland. Eventually, Cage obtained a job at what would be for him a most important and inspirational place, the Cornish School in Seattle, Washington. From several possibilities that Harrison offered him, Cage selected the Cornish one because the school owned a large collection of percussion instruments.[23]

The Cornish School, founded on principles encouraging interdisciplinarity and critical thinking, presented Cage with the perfect environment in which to flourish. He arrived at a time when dance had become increasingly important; Bonnie Bird had begun a programme the previous year with only five students, but among those five were two individuals who would play an important part in the development of Cage's artistic and personal life, Syvilla Fort and Merce Cunningham.

Cage intended one of the first compositions he made at Cornish as a kind of calling card, an indication of his pedigree as a Schoenberg student: the *Metamorphosis* for piano solo. (Cage nearly always used forms of the verb 'make', rather than 'write', to describe his composing.) In addition to his activities at Cornish, he presented several programmes for the Seattle Artists League. Through these events, he interacted with a number of forward-thinking individuals who nurtured his developing ideas on modern music. One of these people, Ralph Gundlach, was Bonnie Bird's husband and a psychology professor at the University of Washington. As part of his research into the emotional effects of music, Gundlach owned some recordings of constant-frequency test tones for the use of recording engineers; these he loaned to Cage, who found use for them in his evolving vision of music.

In addition to music, Cage began articulating his aesthetic ideas with such striking essays as 'The Future of Music: Credo', which Leta E. Miller dates to 1940, close to the end of his time in Seattle.[24] Within its novel design (the actual credo, in small caps, alternates with a lengthier passage of complementary prose), Cage discussed many of his current concerns while taking aim at his former master, Schoenberg, and his insistence on harmony as the primary building block of music:

THE PRESENT METHODS OF WRITING MUSIC, PRINCIPALLY THOSE WHICH EMPLOY HARMONY AND ITS REFERENCE TO PARTICULAR STEPS IN THE FIELD OF SOUND, WILL BE INADEQUATE FOR THE COMPOSER, WHO WILL BE FACED WITH THE ENTIRE FIELD OF SOUND.

And if 'music' struck people as a term that should be reserved for the harmonious art of the past, he added, another phrase could serve: 'organization of sound'. (Cage borrowed the term from Varèse, who later sent a telegram to Cage requesting that he cease using it.[25])

Cage's growing social life was further enlivened by his friendships with two artists from the so-called Northwest School, Mark Tobey and Morris Graves. From Tobey, whose abstract style developed in part from his study of Chinese calligraphy, Cage began thinking deeply about the profound relationship between art and life. He remembered seeing an all-white painting by Tobey and then looking at the sidewalk, finding it as beautiful as the painting: an object made worthy of contemplation simply by changing his attitude of seeing. Cage also recalled that Tobey instructed his students to draw a still life from memory while standing as close to their working surface as possible; the unexpected constraint of physical technique and perspective led to unexpected and novel results.[26]

Graves figures prominently in some of Cage's most hilarious memories. They first met during one of Cage's concerts when, for reasons never explained, Graves exclaimed, 'Jesus in the everywhere!' Later, he and Xenia shared a house with him; on one memorable occasion, Graves expressed his annoyance at a late-night gathering in Cage's rooms that had gone on long enough:

> Xenia never wanted a party to end. Once, in Seattle, when the party we were at was folding, she invited those who were still awake, some of whom we'd only met that evening, to come over to our house. Thus it was that about 3:00 A.M. an Irish tenor was singing loudly in our living room. Morris Graves, who had a suite down the hall, entered ours without knocking, wearing an old-fashioned nightshirt and carrying an elaborately made wooden birdcage, the bottom of which had been removed. Making straight for the tenor, Graves placed the birdcage over his head, said nothing, and left the room. The effect was that of snuffing out a candle. Shortly, Xenia and I were alone.

On another occasion, Graves drove up to a hamburger stand in a car whose seats had been removed and replaced with a table and chairs to resemble a small room; he unrolled a red carpet from the car to the restaurant and, after eating the burger, rolled the carpet back up and drove away.[27]

With the compositions that he made during his two years in Seattle, Cage established for the first time an individual voice in his work. *Imaginary Landscape No. 1* (1939) uses the recordings loaned to him by Gundlach; its scoring includes piano and a percussionist playing a cymbal. It opens with the ghostly and eerily pure sounds of the test tone recordings, soon counterpointed by downward sweeps of the piano strings and a rumbling from the cymbal. This gives way to a solo for muted piano – the pianist strikes the keys with the fingers of one hand while damping the strings inside the instrument with the other hand – that resembles an oracular soliloquy. Soon thereafter, the cymbal punctuates the music at regular intervals, reinforcing the impression of some mysterious, unknowable ritual.

Cage complemented the improvisatory tone of *Imaginary Landscape No. 1* with his composing method: he seemed to plan in advance that his piece would unfold in four sections of nearly equal length, and believed that, once he had constructed this conceptual temporal framework, he could 'fill' it with any sounds he chose. In his next major work of 1939, the *First Construction (in Metal)*, he expanded this idea of rhythmic structure so that the number of musical phrases at the surface level proportionally matched the number of larger musical sections; a collection of short and distinct ideas helped illuminate the rhythmic structure to a limited extent.[28]

In 1940 Cage worked over a period of several months with the dance student Syvilla Fort on her *Bacchanale*, a piece she presented in her graduate recital that June; although specific gestures and positions in her choreography derived from African traditions, Fort tempered the sense of primitivism with other elements clearly related to the modern dance techniques of Martha Graham. Cage's musical response to her work was extraordinary. Following on earlier innovations by Cowell, Cage inserted various materials including weather stripping, screws and bolts into a grand piano; the resulting prepared piano, as he called it, sounded in this instance much like an African marimbula. The structure and sound of Cage's music both matched the modernist posture of Fort's dance and often created an audible articulation of her choreography.[29] The music's driving rhythms marked a new visceral emphasis in Cage's music that would continue through much of the 1940s, and the prepared piano itself functioned as a kind of epiphany in his musical thought; he would employ it on countless occasions in the future.

After Cage's work at the Cornish School, he continued his part-time work at Mills College. Indeed, he joined the faculty briefly during the 1940 academic year; there he began the first of many abortive attempts to establish a kind of research laboratory for the creative use of percussion and electronic instruments, an attempt to bring the forward-thinking predictions of 'The Future of Music: Credo' into reality. He continued to write music for dance and concert works for percussion, notably the 1941 works *Third Construction* and *Double Music* (composed collaboratively with Harrison), and he met such luminaries as Henry Miller and László Moholy-Nagy.

For the 1941 academic year, Moholy-Nagy invited Cage to move to Chicago and teach a course called 'Sound Experiments' at the newly established School of Design. Cage and Xenia moved there and also managed to transport Cage's large percussion instrumentarium. Moholy-Nagy's interest in developing new musical instruments must have made the offer particularly attractive. The course was not well attended, however, and Cage's hope to establish his Center for Experimental Music in Chicago also came to nothing.

Other events, however, bolstered Cage's hopes for the future. In 1942 he began writing occasional pieces for the influential periodical *Modern Music*; his quirky articles no doubt increased his visibility with a number of music professionals. In March of that year, he presented a concert at the Arts Club of Chicago that created a media splash: *Time* magazine published an article filled with photographs. And in May CBS Radio broadcast a Kenneth Patchen play, *The City Wears a Slouch Hat*, which included percussion music by Cage. (His original plan for the incidental music, involving a complicated use of electronic equipment, had to be scrapped.) Although the broadcast had a mixed response, the positive reviews gave him the sense that he was on the right track.

That track led eastward, to New York, where Cage felt certain his fortune would be made. He had met the Surrealist artist Max Ernst in Chicago; Ernst extended an open invitation to Cage and Xenia to visit at the large house on the East River that Ernst shared with Peggy Guggenheim. In June the couple decided to take him up on his offer:

> When Xenia and I came to New York from Chicago, we arrived in the bus station with about twenty-five cents . . . I went to the phone booth in the bus station, put in a nickel, and dialed. Max Ernst answered. He didn't recognize my voice. Finally he said, 'Are you thirsty?' I said, 'Yes.' He said, 'Well, come over tomorrow for cocktails.' I went back to Xenia and told her what had happened. She said, 'Call him back. We have everything to gain and nothing to lose.' I did. He said, 'Oh! It's you. We've been waiting for you for weeks. Your room's ready. Come right over.'[30]

The outlook continued to brighten during their initial time in New York. They met such luminaries as André Breton, Gypsy Rose Lee, Piet Mondrian and Varèse. Cowell, to whom Cage had remained loyal throughout the period of Cowell's incarceration, offered him occasional work substituting for him at the New School for Social Research. And Cage began a fruitful professional relationship the powerful critic Virgil Thomson. Thomson, also well known as the celebrated composer of *Four Saints in Three Acts*, shared Cage's interests in French music and Gertrude Stein; no doubt Thomson's homosexuality also influenced their camaraderie. He helped Cage immeasurably with extremely positive reviews of his music in the *New York Herald Tribune*:

> [Cage's thematic ideas] appear in augmentation, diminution, inversion, fragmentation, and the various kinds of canon. That these procedures do not take over a piece and become its subject, or game, is due to Cage's genius as a musician. He writes music for expressive purposes; and the novelty of his timbres, the logic of his discourse, are used to intensify communication, not as ends in themselves. His work represents, in consequence, not only the most advanced methods now in use anywhere, but original expression of the very highest poetic quality.[31]

Thomson also helped Cage with professional awards later in the 1940s, and asked him to write a book discussing Thomson's life and music.

Unfortunately, troubles – both professional and personal – loomed ahead. Cage's entrepreneurial attempt to arrange a concert at the Museum of Modern Art enraged Peggy Guggenheim, who had promised to pay for the transport of Cage's percussion instruments to New York; she now nullified that arrangement, cancelled a Cage concert scheduled to take place at her own gallery and asked Cage and Xenia to leave her home. Of that episode, Cage remembered sobbing at the feet of Marcel Duchamp, whose serene presence he found strangely comforting.[32]

A greater personal crisis began when Cage became reacquainted with Merce Cunningham, who was now performing with Martha Graham. Whereas formerly Cunningham had liked Cage in the way a talented student likes and admires a favourite professor, the two now found themselves increasingly attracted to each other emotionally and physically. At first Xenia was unaffected by the relationship; in fact, all three became intimately involved for a time.[33] But the relationship soon created an irreparable rift in the marriage. The aftermath of that crisis brought about an equally catastrophic change in Cage's life and art.

3

Non-attachment

Although Cage's initial experiences in New York gave him reason both to despair and celebrate, he soon reached a moment of extreme crisis that threatened both his psyche and his fundamental beliefs about the function of art and the artist. The singular events that made it possible for him to emerge from this critical period also brought about a profound change in his views of life and aesthetics. Within a decade Cage would forge a vital new identity, the one for which he is best known today.

His marriage to Xenia had deteriorated steadily since 1942, when Cage became reacquainted with Merce Cunningham. Cunningham had come to New York expecting to join Martha Graham's dance company, but in addition to performances with her, Cage actively encouraged the young choreographer to strike out on his own. Thus began a series of collaborations to create a type of dance theatre influenced by Graham but more decisively shaped by the striking rhythms of Cage's music, by Cunningham's more lyrical, virtuosic choreography and ultimately by the counterpoint created by the separate artistic concerns of both men.

Credo in us (1942) – a duet for Cunningham and Joseph Campbell's wife, Jean Erdman – is representative. (Campbell, who met Xenia on the West Coast in 1932, made his home available to the Cages during this period and the two couples were good friends.) The dance's music combines Cage's primitive-inspired percussion music with elements of more bourgeois music-making: one performer

Merce Cunningham and John Cage, *c.* 1958.

spins classical records (especially Beethoven and Tchaikovsky) or
simply catches whatever music she can by radio; and extended solo
piano interludes flirt with jazz, boogie-woogie and faux-cowboy
noodling. On the whole, *Credo* offers a satirical critique of American
culture and its cocksure optimism.

Cage found himself increasingly drawn to Merce – not merely as
a diversion from his otherwise comfortable marriage to Xenia, but
as a new, vital relationship with important emotional consequences
of its own. This union – the articulation of creativity and sexuality
Cage found in his companionship with Cunningham – had no real
model. His gay colleagues – above all, Virgil Thomson – represented
a genteel and delicate expression: Thomson's own music, not
surprisingly, was witty, urbane, but extremely reticent, perhaps
prudish. Cage's preferences for explosive, almost pagan rhythm
and his commitment to music for dance, by contrast, suggested
a sensibility much more unabashedly engaged with the body.

Although Cage had begun a lifelong partnership with Cunningham, the transition to that relationship caused him much emotional pain and turmoil; his agonized feelings found voice in various works from this time. In *The Perilous Night* (1943), a substantial five-movement work for prepared piano, the most anguished outcries appear in the faster movements, which bristle with a rhythmically charged angst; Cage said it depicts the sadness of a relationship that becomes unhappy. He and Xenia separated in 1944. His *Four Walls* (written the same year) is an unrelieved elegy of extended minor harmonies for solo (unprepared) piano, around an hour in duration, articulated in the centre by a frightened outcry for solo voice. The music was used for a so-called dance drama by Cunningham, which evoked the psychic breakdown of a married couple.

For some time composers have employed their music to express the difficulties of their lives. These problems cannot always be explicitly identified, of course. Beethoven made a point of linking his own deafness, and the desperation it caused, with his renewed commitment to compose; the great emotional moments of his music – alternately fear, ecstasy, anger or love – confirm this connection again and again.

In the midst of Cage's emotional turmoil, by contrast, music could not provide a source of comfort and self-expression. To his dismay, these passionate outbursts, surely designed to express his feelings and perhaps to gain sympathy for them, fell on the astonished ears of shallow critics who, in the case of *Perilous Night*, were too preoccupied with the unusual sounds of the prepared piano to search any deeper beneath its musical surface. Cage was mortified to know that these critics compared the work to the sound of 'a woodpecker in a church belfry'.[1]

And so Cage needed to find some other relief for his emotional wounds. Cage's marriage with Xenia ended in divorce in 1945; the two remained cordial, but much of his correspondence to her consists of short notes accompanying Cage's regular alimony cheques. He moved to an apartment on the lower east side of Manhattan; his relationship with Cunningham continued to lourish, but the two men elected to keep separate residences until 1970. A 1946 consultation with a psychoanalyst failed to indicate a course of action. Instead Cage found himself increasingly drawn to the spiritual tenets of Eastern philosophy, and in these he found a remarkable way forward in life as well as in art. From a somewhat wilful reading of the Indian aesthetician Ananda Coomaraswamy, Cage claimed that the purpose of art was 'to imitate nature in her manner of operation'. Later, Cage's reciprocal studies with Gita Sarabhai helped acquaint him with Indian aesthetics and its expression, notably the so-called permanent emotions – the heroic, the erotic, the wondrous, the mirthful, sorrow, fear, anger, the odious and tranquillity, to which all the others naturally incline. Three great compositions of that decade – *Sonatas and Interludes for Prepared Piano* (1946–8), *The Seasons* (1947) and the *String Quartet in Four Parts* (1949) – all illustrate his preoccupation with representing these emotions through musical sound.[2]

The *Sonatas and Interludes* are particularly rich in expression. A serious, almost hieratic tone dominates the first sonata; from there, the music traces a journey of wildly divergent moods – alternately playful, sexy, violent – culminating in the extreme reticence of Sonatas 13/14 and the concluding Sonata 16, which suggests a music box quietly playing in some distant reality. Overwhelmingly, however, the *Sonatas and Interludes* espouse an inwardness that is baffling in its extreme neutrality.

This tranquillity can also be linked to a number of Cage's purely aesthetic concerns: his desire to create a temporal structure that would admit a place for unconventional sounds used as musical material, or more broadly his own predilection for the more transparent, evanescent sensibilities of French music as opposed to the grandeur and emotional ardour of German. But it is possible, too, that his negative feelings towards the grand utterances of his own time (Olivier Messiaen, whose *Turangalila-Symphonie* had recently been premiered in the US, was one of the contemporary composers that Cage criticized in a published diatribe against harmony) led him to the quietude of the *Sonatas and Interludes* and informed his frustration that his own concerns and their expression in music had all too often been regarded as frivolous by tacit comparison.

In 1948 Cage made a brief visit to Black Mountain College, near Asheville, North Carolina – he had applied to teach there once before, in 1939, without success. This unusual institution allowed students to design their own curriculum; there were no exams or final grades, and a great emphasis was placed on the arts. In addition students and faculty alike helped to maintain the facility, to farm its land and to work together as a democratic whole in all matters that concerned the school's administration and development. While many of its faculty and alumni have noted that Black Mountain anticipated the freer, counterculture attitude of the 1960s, it is equally arguable that the school's democratic premise was based on the assumption that both students and faculty held a similar worldview that allowed such governance to be possible. In practice, however, a lack of consensus on such issues resulted in a great splintering among its members, which sometimes reached the level of full-scale ideological schisms.

Cage's first visit lasted six days; it took place in early April and formed part of a longer performance tour that he arranged on Cunningham's behalf.[3] The Black Mountain visit occurred at a propitious moment for the school: musical activities had diminished as the result of important faculty departures, and the community had also become interested in cultivating contemporary dance. In addition to his activities accompanying Cunningham, Cage performed the premiere of the *Sonatas and Interludes*, which had just been completed the month before. He also captured the attention of the college community with his legendary charm and charisma; his holistic philosophy – that art served to integrate the personality of its maker and, by extension, performers and audiences – resonated powerfully with the Black Mountain zeitgeist. He and Cunningham were paid only with room and board, though Cage would later fondly remember that artworks and additional food were given as gifts before their departure.

On the basis of this first successful visit, Cage negotiated a longer tenure during the 1948 summer session, where he taught a course in the structure of music twice a week. But by this time one of the music faculty, the harpsichordist and pianist Erwin Bodky, had returned to Black Mountain with the expectation of restoring its music department to prominence. Bodky, who taught courses on both general keyboard literature and the Beethoven piano sonatas, was chagrined by Cage's resolutely modern views. The problem was further compounded because Cage's invitation issued from the art department (specifically through the Bauhaus artist Joseph Albers); technically, therefore, Cage was not an official member of the music programme at all.

For his part, Cage exacerbated the situation through his activities, which he portrayed in a consciously non-elitist manner. Perhaps as a goad to Bodky's thoroughly classical (and often Germanic) recital offerings, Cage mounted what he dubbed the Amateur Festival of the Music of Erik Satie, a series of half-hour evening concerts on Mondays, Wednesdays and Fridays, some of which took place in Cage's modest cabin. He also presented a polemical lecture, 'Defense of Satie', in which he claimed that Beethoven's emphasis on harmony and rhetoric had derailed and indeed nearly destroyed the healthy course of Western music.[4]

Reminiscences of this controversy vary widely; some recall that the difference of opinion carried little import, while others considered it a full-scale attack on authority and tradition. Surely it pointed to the rift not only between German and French aesthetics, but also between the academic, professional musical community and Cage's so-called untrained approach – the latter, by refusing to acknowledge the wisdom of longstanding tradition, argued for something then unthinkable: that people could seriously explore the creation of new music through completely different routes than those found within the academy. (Cage conveniently underplayed his tendency to espouse his pedigree on such occasions.)

In 1948, too, Cage made the acquaintance of M. C. Richards, an extraordinary writer and artist – and one of the most important women in Cage's creative circle. Richards would translate into English Antonin Artaud's seminal *Theatre and Its Double* (1938; New York, 1958), a text that Cage later described as fundamental to his concepts of theatre and art generally. He also met Paul and Vera Williams, students who later supported him through the commission of the electronic tape piece *Williams Mix* (1952) and, perhaps more importantly, through the establishment of a cooperative community at Stony Point, New York, the Gate Hill Community, to which Cage would move in 1954.

Cage's growing national reputation also made other personal developments possible. Two awards, a Guggenheim and a grant from the National Institute of Arts and Letters (awarded in April and May 1949, respectively), enabled him to visit Europe as well. In Paris he performed with Cunningham, studied the works of Satie and played the *Sonatas and Interludes* for Messiaen's private composition class. In Italy he attended and reviewed the 23rd Festival of the International Society for Contemporary Music and the First Congress for Dodecaphonic Music: these professional contacts bolstered Cage's awareness of contemporary music and his reputation in an increasingly international community.

He also introduced himself to Pierre Boulez. The two met at a time in their lives when both were interested in an approach to music that eschewed subjectivity. Adopting an adversarial stance to the nineteenth-century music tradition, Boulez described his

David Tudor, 1950s.

work with composition as a kind of research; Cage's tendency,
in his writings, to categorize music into objective, quantifiable
components such as amplitude and duration also appealed to
Boulez's quasi-scientific mentality. Indeed Cage would later
characterize his music as experimental, a music whose outcome
could not be known in advance.

Cage also helped the younger composer find publishers for
the works of his early maturity that would bring him his first international acclaim, in particular the aggressive second piano sonata.
After they parted, the two maintained a lively correspondence. Cage
worked ceaselessly to create professional opportunities for Boulez.
He even helped produce the US premiere of Boulez's sonata, which
was finally performed by David Tudor. Tudor, whom Cage met
through the former's work as an accompanist for Jean Erdman, was

a phenomenal pianist and composer whose abilities would make Cage's later music possible.

Although Cage often remarked that Boulez's ideas about music were novel and helpful to him, their friendship was not merely professional, but affectionate as well:

> My dear Pierre,
> Your letter has just arrived here at home. I cannot tell you how overjoyed I was to get it. Without news of you I am without news of music, and you know I love music with all my heart.[5]

This letter suggests a fundamental difference in the way the two composers understood the role of subjectivity in music. Boulez's music expressed an antagonistic, belligerent defiance towards nineteenth-century music, while Cage's music usually suggested temperance but by no means a wholesale denial of expression.

In due time Cage made other American friends who were both profoundly influenced by him and profoundly nurturing to him in

Morton Feldman and John Cage, 1950s.

return. Morton Feldman, who had studied composition with Wallingford Riegger and Stefan Wolpe, met Cage as they left a concert by the New York Philharmonic on 26 January 1950; both had come to hear the Webern symphony, which had been viciously booed by the audience, and were uninterested in hearing the tamer offerings that followed. (The concert included Beethoven's 'Emperor' concerto and the *Symphonic Dances* of Rachmaninoff.)

Feldman amazed Cage because he wrote the kind of new music Cage admired, but seemed to do so effortlessly, as if by pure instinct. The younger composer soon became Cage's neighbour in a building at Grand Street and Monroe overlooking the East River. He remembered late-night conversations with Cage and the visual artists of the day at the Cedar Bar, conversations that took place every evening 'for five years of [their] lives'.[6] In his single-minded cultivation of musical composition, Feldman became Cage's most famous younger contemporary – a new-music composer's composer, one who arguably surpassed his mentor.

A short time later, Cage began teaching a sixteen-year-old boy named Christian Wolff, whose father – a publisher – oversaw the Bollingen Series of Princeton University Press. Because Wolff received his lessons free of charge, he gave Cage gifts of books from his father's press. This community expanded still further during the course of a performance trip with Cunningham to the western United States in April 1951. There, Cage met Earle Brown and his wife, Carolyn; Carolyn joined Cunningham's dance company, while her husband, a composer, allied himself strongly with Cage and later with Tudor, Feldman and Wolff. Together the five composers became known as the New York Experimental School.

One of the most important events during this time was Cage's acquaintance with the works of Japanese scholar Daisetsu Teitaro Suzuki. Suzuki's self-proclaimed mission was to bring to the West a thorough understanding of Eastern philosophy and particularly Zen

Buddhism. Towards this end, his writings often took account of Western ideas, which allowed him to make meaningful connections with his intended audience.

It is not clear how Cage first became aware of Suzuki. (He sold off his own library, book by book, during the 1950s.) The early writings of the British philosopher Alan Watts, heretofore unexamined by Cage scholarship, provide a clue. In one short volume published in 1948, Watts cites the importance of Suzuki and includes references to Suzuki's work as well as another book that Cage himself named as an important influence, *The Huang Po Doctrine of Universal Mind*.[7]

There can be no doubt that Cage knew the Watts source because he adapted a passage from it for his own 'Lecture on Nothing' (*c.* 1949–50), the earliest text in which Cage began to demonstrate a conscious desire to shape his own aesthetic by appropriating images and themes from Zen. Watts's original quotation refers to Zen's paradoxical employment of 'the normal *structure* of the Buddhist religion': 'For pure life expresses itself within and through structure. Life without structure is unseen; it is the unmanifested Absolute. But structure without life is dead, and religion has altogether too much of this death.' Cage, by contrast, modifies the quotation and includes it as part of a longer discussion of the term 'structure'; in this context, however, structure refers to the composition of a whole – a piece of music or, indeed, the 'Lecture on Nothing' itself – as a concatenation of smaller, constituent parts: 'Structure without life is dead. But Life without structure is un-seen. Pure life expresses itself within and through structure. Each moment is absolute, alive and significant.'[8] Perhaps Cage had access to this source through his continuing contact with Joseph Campbell; the book was in Campbell's library. In any case, Cage soon embraced Suzuki as his most important authority on Zen. By early 1950 he mentioned in a letter to Boulez that Suzuki's works were about to be republished.[9]

However Cage first encountered Suzuki's ideas, his actual contact with him was as influential as it was mysterious. For although Cage claimed to have studied with Suzuki for two or three years beginning in the late 1940s, Suzuki arrived in America only in late summer 1950 and did not give his first lecture at Columbia University until March 1951. His first official class took place in the spring of 1952, and auditors have verified that Cage attended both this course and another in the autumn.[10]

Cage was ever mindful of his story as an artist, frequently legitimizing it with his name-dropping of important figures; his quasi-mythic story of his studies with Arnold Schoenberg is a typical example. Suzuki seemed to offer Cage what Schoenberg had done in the late 1930s and early '40s: a way of creating a new sense of an aesthetic and an authority that would lend further prestige to Cage's evolving story of himself: one that tapped into the multicultural vogue he had so often earlier celebrated, but one leading to radically different results.

Suzuki's remarks touched on themes that Cage had already embraced in other contexts. One, surely, was his paradoxical rejection of grandeur, of rhetoric. The expression of his own ego, so typical of Beethoven, was repugnant to him; but what is music other than the self-expression of the artist's mind? Suzuki taught that the ego, through its process of embracing things that pleased it and rejecting the rest, closed itself off from the experiences of the world *in toto*. Therefore, one had to eliminate a bondage to judgements in order to apprehend the totality of existence.[11]

The philosopher's description of events and their relationships proved even more important. As Cage recalled,

In the course of a lecture last winter at Columbia, Suzuki said that there was a difference between oriental thinking and European thinking, that in European thinking things are seen as causing one another and having effects, whereas in oriental thinking this seeing of cause and effect is not emphasized but instead one makes an identification with what is here and now.

He then spoke of two qualities: unimpededness and interpenetration. Unimpededness is seeing that in all of space each thing and each human being is at the center and furthermore that each one being at the center is the most honored one of all. Interpenetration means that each one of the most honored ones of all is moving out in all directions penetrating and being penetrated by every other one no matter what the time or what the space. So that when one says that there is no cause and effect, what is meant is that there are an incalculable infinity of causes and effects, that in fact each and every thing in all of time and space is related to each and every other thing in all of time and space. This being so there is no need to cautiously proceed in dualistic terms of success and failure or the beautiful and the ugly or good and evil, but rather simply to walk on 'not wondering', to quote Meister Eckhart, 'Am I right or doing something wrong.'[12]

Cage never specifically cited any of Suzuki's writings, though he mentioned that Suzuki recommended he read the writings of Zhuangzi (Kwang-tze); specific quotations of this Taoist writer can be found in *Silence*. In addition, ample documentation supports Cage's approval of a specific text: *The Huang Po Doctrine of Universal Mind*, which had been translated by Chu Ch'an (John Blofeld) and published by the Buddhist Society of London in 1947. Indeed, this book provides an unusually succinct primer of what Zen Buddhism entails. To be sure, its guidance is ambiguous, since one of Zen's major tenets is that it cannot be adequately conveyed through words. But words, like music, can help people approach ideas and feelings that are ultimately impossible to transmit exactly from one person to another.

First, Zen requires an unspoken understanding between a teacher and pupil; the aim of this understanding is to apprehend Mind – an intangible substance that is common to all sentient beings but which cannot be described or measured: if, for instance, one says Mind is absolutely pure, that statement implies the existence of something else that it is absolutely filthy; if one describes it as infinite, the proposition implies that something else exists which is only finite. Therefore the sorts of things apprehended with the senses – emotions, intellectual ideas, physiological urges, even a sense of individual self – are only momentary phenomena that have no overall importance. But Zen enlightenment does not come from ignoring these phenomena, by not thinking, feeling, eating – but rather by engaging in these activities without any feelings of attachment or revulsion. This neither/nor mindset, as Blofeld makes clear in supplementary commentary, is dispassionate but by no means apathetic or uncaring.

Someone who can respond in this manner to the phenomena around her realizes that Mind was never something to look for in the first place. Hsi Yun, the supposed author of the *Doctrine*, offers the following anecdote:

> Suppose a warrior, who did not realise he was wearing a pearl (which he thought to be lost) on his forehead, were to seek for it elsewhere; though he were to traverse the whole universe, he would never find it. But if a knowing fellow were to point it out to him, he would immediately realise that it was still in its old place.[13]

Thus enlightenment comes suddenly and completely; it has the sensation of an afterthought: good works do not hasten its arrival and neither does meditation or assiduous study of venerated texts. These activities have their place, but they are no more means to an end than breathing or brushing your teeth; they are simply what you do. In that important sense, then, there is nothing magical about enlightenment, and that in turn demonstrates how Zen runs counter to the quasi-mystical, fantastic sense of art that Cage appropriated, for instance, from the writings of the medieval Christian mystic Meister Eckhart. From this point onward, Cage's aesthetic would be permeated by a delight in the everyday, the non-fetishizing of objects and the celebration of activity as the most important creative act of all.

While at Grand Street, Cage received something of critical importance to his newly formed aesthetic; as a token of gratitude for one of his lessons, Wolff gave him an English-language edition of the I Ching, or *Book of Changes* (Princeton, 1950), just at the time that he was completing his *Concerto for Prepared Piano and Chamber Orchestra* (1950–51).

The ancient Oriental book is a series of commentaries on 64 distinct states of being, each represented by a hexagram in which each of the six lines is either solid or divided in the middle – the 64 states are in constant flux. Any hexagram thus offers a 'snapshot' of the momentary state of the universe, which is constantly changing to another. The commentaries are designed to advise those who would consult the book as an oracular tool.

To use the I Ching in this manner, one formulates a question and then tosses three two-sided coins six times. The result of each toss symbolizes a solid or broken line; for instance, a toss yielding two tails and a head corresponds to a solid line, while one of two heads and a tail corresponds to a broken line. The user takes this information and constructs a hexagram, drawing the lines from the bottom to the top.

Tosses of three heads or three tails signify a further nuance to the changing nature of the 64 states, a so-called changing line that has already begun the process of transformation into its opposite: thus, three tails correspond to an unbroken line that has begun to change into a broken one, while three heads signify a broken line that will change into an unbroken one. To extend the snapshot analogy, a hexagram with no changing lines is analogous to a photograph of a car *momentarily at rest*; a hexagram with moving lines is analogous to a snapshot of a car *in motion*. If the user generates a hexagram with one or more changing lines, he continues the oracle-obtaining process by drawing a *second* hexagram in which he renders each moving line as its opposite. In such cases, the answer for the question asked refers to two specific hexagrams.

Cage once admitted that there had been a time when he consulted the I Ching often as an oracle, whenever he had any problem in his life.[14] For the purposes of his composition, however, he used it as a kind of rarefied number generator. Writing music thus became something other than the customary working out of sonic ideas that originated in a composer's mind. Instead, Cage devised for many of his pieces an elaborate series of questions that described every aspect from the most general to the most specific. For each question, he formulated a number of possible answers, each of which corresponded to one or a range of the 64 I Ching hexagram numbers. When this precompositional design was in place, he tossed three coins six times to generate the hexagrams, and thus had no direct influence on the answers selected for each of the questions. Cage now had a response to the question Schoenberg posed during the counterpoint class, which he adapted to this new situation: the principle involving compositional solutions involves the questions that are asked.

Cage's interest in Zen brought about a decisive sea change in his life and thought. His methods led to the gradual abandonment of his own taste in the making of his compositions. The *Concerto for Prepared Piano and Chamber Orchestra* exemplified his new aesthetic orientation.

In the concerto he had already moved towards eliminating his own compositional intervention by arraying his pre-composed materials in charts: simple, game-like moves around the various cells of the charts determined the unfolding of these materials in the time span of the composition, resulting in an unusual assortment of sounds and continuity. For the last movement, Cage used the

I Ching to generate hexagram numbers corresponding to these moves, removing himself from the process even further.

The expressive profile of the piece is, perhaps, more apparent than the compositional technique that Cage used would imply. He imagined the piece as a confrontation between the piano and orchestra, but of a very different sort from the tradition of the Romantic piano concertos. Whereas in those works, the piano was cast as hero – sometimes struggling with, sometimes inspiring, the orchestra – in Cage's concerto the struggle was between self-expression, rhapsody, interiority (the piano) and a blank, impassive existence for the orchestra. The orchestra was not so much a cruel force opposing the piano's individuality but more akin to a Zen master instructing the student with a combination of paradox, nonsense or occasional outright violence. As the concerto unfolds, the piano gradually abandons its figurations and improvisatory flourishes, until finally – in the last movement – both piano and orchestra are in accord.

This unity between piano and orchestra appears particularly in persistent passages in which neither plays. Silence here becomes something other than a means for dramatic pause or punctuation, but rather approaches thematic significance. It signifies the unity of purpose or of understanding between piano and orchestra, but it also enfolds the audience itself into this understanding: silence becomes a window to everyday reality that opens and closes periodically during the movement, and the audience attends to sounds in the hall that have nothing whatsoever to do with the sounds issuing from Cage's own imagination. Gone is the rhythmic excitement that marked so many of Cage's works up to that point. And the absence of that rhythmic drive also tends to smooth out the gestures of the music and its expressive surface, to transform them into something unfamiliar and inscrutable.

Even so, it is a mistake to think that Cage's embrace of Zen meant that his music was to have some sort of ethereal, otherworldly sensibility, for in Zen one attains enlightenment suddenly, by realizing that everyday life *is* enlightenment once one lets go of his passions, his desires, his endless categorization. Thus nothing is excluded from this music. In Cage's first fully composed chance piece, *Music of Changes* (1951), he exulted in the infinite variety of what 'everything' could mean. He also employed charts in this piece: one for rhythms, one for pitches, one for dynamics and articulation, one showing how many musical layers might be superimposed on one another. The I Ching determined how every aspect of these charts interacted with each other to create the finished work. In its way, the febrile kineticism of the piece recalls the restless aggression of Boulez's second piano sonata – Boulez and Cage were in close contact during the composition of this piece and shared certain ideas about sound worlds and gesture. Boulez's thoughts led to the forbidding *Structures*, a highly organized piece whose precompositional structure was so fully worked out in advance that it almost wrote itself and led its composer to look for more flexible creative intervention in the course of composition. By contrast, Cage felt that the precompositional systems of *Music of Changes* reduced him to the status of a kind of clerical worker dutifully accomplishing his appointed tasks but remaining strangely unfulfilled by the outcome. He himself referred to the work later as a Frankenstein monster:[15] it was not so much that the monster mastered its maker, but that the monster was unable to amicably cohabitate, to interact, with the world around it.

Colleagues and critics began to find Cage's embrace of chance increasingly difficult to endorse. Already by May 1951 Boulez showed indications of this difficulty in his correspondence: while he remained cordial and supportive of Cage's music, he confessed that the works of Feldman and Wolff did not interest him. By December Boulez wrote to commend Cage for the direction his music was taking in *Music of Changes*, with one exception:

The only thing, forgive me, which I am not happy with, is the method of absolute chance (*by tossing the coins*). On the contrary, I believe that chance must be extremely controlled . . . I believe that it would be possible to direct the phenomenon of the automatism of chance . . . which I mistrust as a facility that is not absolutely necessary.[16]

Cage's writings from around the same time reflect Zen in various ways and to varying degrees. He retained those elements of Indian philosophy that still resonated with his aesthetic – for instance, although Zen could not acknowledge any notions of duality, Cage continued to hold the view (gained from Gita Sarabhai) that art should sober and quiet the mind, thus rendering it susceptible to divine influences. Other references, for example to Meister Eckhart and tranquillity, remained as well. Nevertheless, Cage's prose began to reflect the importance of Zen within his aesthetics.

In the 'Lecture on Nothing', for example, Cage began to refer to the concept of 'nothing' as something similar to the void of Zen or of Taoism, as in the classic remark 'I have nothing to say and I am saying it and that is poetry as I need it.' Remarks against possessing anything – sounds, music and so on – correspond strongly with the Zen principle of non-attachment. But Cage's continuing allegiance to the notion of a temporal structure in music rejected the sudden enlightenment that the *Huang Po Doctrine* espouses. By contrast, Cage emphasized the idea of a continual progression without end:

Here we are now a little bit after the beginning of the fourth large part of this talk. More and more we have the feeling that I am getting nowhere. Slowly, as the talk goes on, slowly, we have the feeling that we are getting nowhere. That is a pleasure which will continue. If we are irritated, it is not a pleasure. Nothing is not a pleasure if one is irritated, but suddenly, it is a pleasure, and then more and more it is not irritating (and then more and more and slowly). Originally we were nowhere; and now, again, we are having the pleasure of being slowly nowhere. If anybody is sleepy, let him go to sleep. Here we are now at the beginning of the third unit of the fourth large part of this talk. More and more I have the feeling that we are getting nowhere.[17]

Only in 'Lecture on Something' (*c.* 1950) did Cage begin to explore the implications of nondualism in his aesthetics: 'The important question is what is it that is not just beautiful but also ugly, not just good, but also evil, not just true, but also illusion.'[18] Using remarks about Feldman's music as a point of departure, Cage advocated a reception to music that accepts everything that happens, without the need of looking for a single overarching plan that describes it.

Cage's second trip to Black Mountain, in August 1952, was by no means the only evidence of his continuing impact at the school after 1948. His *String Quartet in Four Parts* was premiered there in 1950 and Tudor, who taught and worked with Merce Cunningham during those years, performed *Music of Changes* at the school.

Although Cage did not teach a class during this second visit and was present for only a month, his activities during that time had, perhaps, even greater influence for the students and his own future. His engagement with a new aesthetic was particularly tangible in an all-night reading of the *Huang Po Doctrine*. But a Zen sensibility was also apparent in the so-called *Black Mountain Piece* (1952), which responded in part to Artaud's thoughts about the basic equivalence of all theatrical components – gesture, light, text and design. In its single performance, the event comprised a rich variety of different activities meant to be understood as an artistic whole: among other contributions, Cage recited the Bill of Rights, the Declaration of Independence and a lecture of Meister Eckhart; Cunningham danced (sometimes joined extemporaneously by a dog); M. C. Richards and Charles Olson read poetry; and the artist Robert

Rauschenberg (another recent acquaintance from New York) performed his old recordings with an antiquated phonograph and displayed his paintings that were completely white and contained no representation of any object. The audience was arranged so that the performers did their work around them, and thus the usual senses of hierarchy between performers and audience and focus points of attention were further obliterated.

Following closely on the heels of *Music of Changes* came an altogether different piece, one of the most famous and misunderstood of all Cage's works, *4'33"* (1952). Like all of his pieces up to this point, it involved creating musical phrases one after another until the work was finished, but in this instance each and every phrase was silent: Cage literally built the piece out of silent rhythmic values, concatenating them to form the whole. The title is nothing more than a description of total duration in minutes and seconds: no poetic title, no hint as to content or aesthetic.

At its first performance on 29 August in Woodstock, New York, the audience was understandably bewildered. Was Cage ridiculing them with the ultimate Dadaist joke, a piece of music in which they were invited to attend to nothing at all? 'Good people of Woodstock, let's run these people out of town', one man urged.[19]

But of course there *were* sounds going on in the work – very quiet ones: air moving about, the breathing of the audience, their physical rustling in chairs and with programmes, squeaking chairs, and – as if heaven-sent – a terrific thunderstorm outside. Cage had finally found a way to let sounds be sounds, unmediated by the imagination of the composer or the annoying burden of a history of prior music that conditioned its listeners like Pavlovian automatons.

As Cage admitted, he was partially emboldened to create *4'33"* through the example of Rauschenberg's white paintings. But Rauschenberg's canvases were objects, brought into existence through the artist's decision to cover the surface with a single colour that had no pattern, no representation. Cage had not created a silent piece in which the performer pretended to play, which might be the closest thing to Rauschenberg's white paintings that can be imagined, but rather placed a frame around mobile, everyday life.

Naturally this was an extreme statement, one that could scarcely be repeated. Cage knew that he would have to continue writing music in order to keep his promise to Schoenberg. But how would he do this and yet continue to honour the extraordinary discovery of *4'33"*? The answer came through new kinds of notation and new kinds of freedom for the performer, gifts that he felt could allow performers to escape their own tastes and prejudices and experience sounds for themselves in the way the audience could experience ambience and unintended sound in *4'33"*.

Music for Piano 4–19 (1954) extended the idea of chance music to a new level. The performer chooses the tempo, the order of pages, even what music to omit and what to include. Thus the overall profile of such music could be radically different each time it was performed. Cage called such music indeterminate in order to distinguish it from such chance compositions as *Music of Changes*, which afforded the performer far fewer freedoms.

Colleagues and critics began to decry Cage's growing commitment to chance with increasing vigour. Boulez expressed his disdain in an essay, 'Alea', while a *New York Times* critic pronounced a Tudor recital that included *4'33"* (along with *Music of Changes* and works by Brown and Wolff) as 'an evening of singularly graceless and uninspired music . . . hollow, sham, pretentious Greenwich Village exhibitionism'.[20] Later that year, Cage travelled to Germany and the important new music festival at Donaueschingen; there, he and Tudor performed *34'46.776" for Two Pianists* (1954) which, though offered in a shortened version, did not please an audience who probably had been expecting music more akin to the *Sonatas and Interludes*. Cage was undoubtedly affected by this experience; he did not return to Donaueschingen until 1972. And his friendship with Thomson reached an impasse due to Thomson's duplicity regarding the book he asked Cage to write (without Cage's knowledge, he was also working with Kathleen O'Donnell Hoover on a biography) and the two composers' increasing disinterest in each other's music.[21]

Cage turned 46 in 1958. By this time his reputation in New York had been long established, principally through his music for percussion and prepared piano, and his exploration of chance and indeterminacy had earned him both criticism and accolades from critics in classical music and modern dance. And so it was that Cage's friends in the art world moved to organize a celebration of his work. The Stable Gallery exhibited his manuscripts as art – with good reason – in early May, while the artists Rauschenberg and Jasper Johns joined with the film director and producer Emile de Antonio to produce a grand concert in New York's Town Hall on 15 May 1958.

Billed as the Twenty-five Year Retrospective of the Work of John Cage, this concert pointed out, more forcefully than ever, the incredible conflicts that Cage would soon experience by liberating musicians to hear sounds as sounds themselves. In the premiere of the *Concert for Piano and Orchestra* (1958) he had given his players

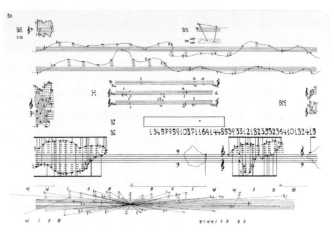

John Cage, *Concert for Piano and Orchestra* (1958), excerpt of piano part.

unimagined freedoms. The notation of the solo part burgeoned with new kinds of graphic symbols and designs – Cage entrusted Tudor with this challenging part. The orchestra parts, by contrast, gave musicians licence to interpret the meaning of different-sized note heads, to add extra musical sounds at specified places, even to perform the individual pages of their parts in any ordering they wished.

Faced with such luxuriant freedoms, some of the performers behaved as one might expect musicians who live and die by their ability to render notated music into sound would behave: they refused to take Cage's music seriously and ended up playing whatever they felt like: jazz riffs, favourite orchestral excerpts, whatever occurred to and amused them.

And yet Cage behaved as responsibly as any composer would to prepare for the event. He met with all the musicians separately and learned the limits of what they could do, seeking to get from them as many new sounds as possible. He probably erred, however, by assuming that the musicians would take the experience of these consultations into the performance, and explore – along with him and his companions – the staggering possibility of sound coming into its own.

Reporting on the event for the *New York Times* the next day, Ross Parmenter said that the *Concert* 'presented some of the craziest mixed-up sounds ever heard on a concert platform'; he noted that some audience members made their own sounds to urge the piece to its conclusion.[22] The wilder *Williams Mix* he dubbed thoroughly entertaining as a result of its brevity. Some of the audience, then, had been no more transformed than some of the musicians had been.

For a time after this event, Cage largely preferred working only with musicians and performers that he knew. His music had not yet liberated people from their own habits and prejudices. Sounds had been released from the indomitable ego of a composer with a message to communicate, but were still subject to the abuse of countless people who did not know how to care about a new music without an explicit intention, gesture and rhetoric. 'My problems', Cage lamented, 'have become social, not musical.'[23]

Late that summer, Cage attended the Brussels World Fair and taught at the renowned Darmstadt summer course for new music. His reception on these occasions was mixed. Surely the force of his personality and charisma helped to advance his cause: he became friends with many emerging composers of the time including Luciano Berio, Karlheinz Stockhausen, Henri Pousseur, Bruno Maderna and Luc Ferrari.

But these composers soon realized that Cage's project was one that threatened the autonomy of the composer and the heritage of the art music tradition. For he regarded a composer's creative intention as non-essential and, indeed, counterproductive; he wanted to eradicate the past, not with the angry violence of Boulez, but with a kind of nonchalance that must have struck many as apathetic or simply naive.

While at Darmstadt, he responded to criticism quite forcefully in 'Communication', a famous lecture that consists principally of questions. Some of Cage's questions seem to refer to the hegemony of twelve-note thinking that had overtaken the summer course. But other questions, more akin to the dialogues of Zen or Taoism, probably had a greater impact, for Cage took care to have them translated into German in such a way that they seemed to be frankly confrontational. For example, the questions 'Why don't they keep their ears open and their mouths shut? Are they stupid?' was rendered into German as 'Why don't you [*Sie*] keep your ears open and your mouths shut? Are you stupid?'[24] In short, Cage had thrown down the gauntlet; in the next decade, he would pursue the implications of indeterminacy to unimagined extremes.

4

Eminence

In 1960 Cage was poised to become the best-known American composer after Aaron Copland, and arguably the best-known American composer to the world at large. Copland's dominance in American musical life had diminished in the early 1950s when rumours about his Communist sympathies led to the cancellation of a performance of his *Lincoln Portrait* and he was subpoenaed to testify before the House Un-American Activities Committee in the us Congress; although he emerged relatively unscathed from the experience, his turn away from the populist works that had cemented his reputation in the 1940s made him less prominent.[1] Other composers such as Arnold Schoenberg, Paul Hindemith and Kurt Weill – though each had become naturalized us citizens – were never wholly embraced by the native sons of their adopted country. Leonard Bernstein became increasingly known as a conductor, and his unabashed alchemy of popular and classical idioms bemused those critics who could have helped establish his well-deserved reputation as one of the country's most original voices.

Perhaps Americans also continued to be spellbound by the most famous composer still alive and residing in Cage's birthplace, Los Angeles: Igor Stravinsky. While it is true that Stravinsky's most recent music made little impression on the general public, his reputation – above all, for the *Firebird* and the notorious *Rite of Spring* – instilled a stereotypical image of what a composer ought to be: a glamorous and mysterious artist who knew everyone worth knowing and travelled to every city worth visiting. With the help of his able amanuensis, Robert Craft, Stravinsky kept himself in the public view with a series of highly entertaining conversation books that perpetuated this image.

Like Stravinsky, Cage was also glamorous and he knew how well charismatic charm could advance a career. Yet in other respects he was a most unlikely candidate for the game he would soon play so well. For one thing, Cage cheerfully denied that intentionality was a desirable trait for a composer, that indeed anyone could do what he was doing if they only decided to take the time necessary to do it. And despite his fondness for pointing out his tutelage with Schoenberg, he never failed to mention the master's criticism that guaranteed his failure: that Cage's inability to cope with harmony would ultimately defeat him.

Cage's music had long seemed to stretch the boundaries of what could be acceptable as music. Much of his new work shocked people who, assaulted by a barrage of unusual sounds, began to wonder whether Cage's seriousness was a colossal joke carried out at their expense. Indeed, such works as *Water Music* (1952) employed a variety of props, including a deck of cards and a duck call; it seemed less like music or avant-garde art than an absurdist vaudeville.

And Cage had other quirks, too. His move in 1954 to a kind of commune in rural Stony Point, New York – some 40 miles from New York City – had given him an urge to satisfy his thirst for nature through walks in the woods, during which he became interested in the mushrooms that he found growing about. An early attempt to impress his friends with the pleasures of organic food led to a notorious repast at which Cage served his guests poisonous hellebore, which he had mistaken for skunk cabbage. Everyone who ate it became ill; Cage, who had eaten the most and was violently ill, had to be rushed to hospital and have his stomach pumped. His doctor told everyone that he would have died otherwise. With his usual enterprise, he set about finding yet another authority figure,

Cage gathering mushrooms in Grenoble, France, 1972.

one who could guide him in the cultivation of this new passion: eventually he reached a man named Guy Nearing.[2]

In the process, Cage began a lifelong love affair with mushrooms; he made much of the fact that the dictionary entries for 'mushroom' and 'music' are so close together. Around 1954 he had written an amusing short essay in which he used the discussion of mushrooms and mushroom hunting as a foil for discussing the then-current state of new music. He imagined that the sounds of spores dropping on the earth might somehow be amplified so they could be heard and enjoyed as music.[3]

He flaunted this hobby in ways that must have seemed unimaginable for other composers of the time: he appeared, for instance, on an Italian tv quiz show, *Lascia o radoppia* – a kind of *$64,000 Question* – as an expert on mushrooms, ultimately walking away with the grand prize of 4,000 lire (about $6,000 at the time). Back in America, he wangled an article from a food writer for *Vogue*, who trekked to Cage's digs to report on his food sources and his cooking.[4] (An avid gourmet, he was particularly fond of French cooking, having discovered it through the work of Julia Child.) In January 1960 Cage appeared on the popular American television show *I've Got a Secret*, performing in utter seriousness the humorous *Water Walk* (1959); the audience seemed to laugh loudest twice, when Cage immersed a small gong in water and when he drank what appeared to be Scotch and soda.

In other words, Cage began to harness the gigantic machines of mass culture to do what more esteemed composers could not – expose himself to the public in an unchallenging and often ingratiating way. Consider, by contrast, the well-known essay by Milton Babbitt, 'Who Cares If You Listen?' (originally titled by its author as 'The Composer as Specialist'), which argued that the university supplied the last great hope for the furtherance of truly important new music, and that university composers (like Babbitt himself) would do well to isolate themselves from the general public in much the same way that physicists or mathematicians share their findings with their own small circle of colleagues. Babbitt's intellect – above all, his innovative research in music theory – was not lost on Cage, and he knew how to deflect it immediately: 'He looks like a musicologist', he wryly observed to Pierre Boulez in 1950.[5]

Like many composers of his time, Cage also began teaching. Unlike many others, however, he taught at The New School for Social Research, where Henry Cowell had taught before him. Cage's students for his Structure of Music course included a handful of people who today are better known as artists than musicians. These individuals – including Dick Higgins, George Brecht, Al Hansen and Alison Knowles – became affiliated with a community of other artists called Fluxus. Like Cage, they believed that fine art could be made from whatever they found around them. In fact, Cage insisted during the course of his classes that his students perform their new works after composing them and further stipulated that they use only materials available to them in the classroom. Fluxus artists created works that relied heavily on the everyday as a site for art. Knowles, for instance, thought of all her works as music, but her pieces often had nothing to do with typical musical sounds whatever – her *Proposition* (1962) consists of a single sentence: 'Make a salad.' Another New School student, Allan Kaprow, staged the elaborate *18 Happenings in Six Parts*, influenced in no small measure by Cage's own event at Black Mountain College. Unlike his teacher, however, Kaprow insisted on the audience behaving in certain ways at certain times, which Cage disliked. Of the event, Carolyn Brown recalled that 'It was a bit like being in a kinder-garten for half-wits.'[6]

The friction between Cage and Kaprow indicates a richly varied discourse between teacher and student. Dick Higgins, who famously described in Cage's classes the 'sense he gave that "anything goes", at least potentially', confessed that he found Cage's detailed descriptions of chance and indeterminacy 'terribly old-fashioned', more akin to 'legal documents' than to the practical advice Cage gave about student compositions.[7] By contrast, Brecht shared many of Cage's interests in Zen Buddhism and his notebooks bear witness to a deep engagement with Cage's ideas that, nevertheless, took the younger artist in a very different direction.[8] Such divergent interactions characterized Fluxus generally, for Fluxus resolutely rejected all kinds of definition and systematization.

Cage's other class at the New School concerned mushroom identification. With Nearing, he formed the New York Mycological Society in 1962. Cage and his mycophilic friends made regular field trips to look for fungi on Saturdays and Sundays; indeed, for a time Cage actually became a purveyor of gourmet mushrooms for a fashionable New York restaurant.[9] As a result of Cage's devotion, he received an award from the North American Mycological Society in 1964. He used his mushroom hunting with the New York Myco-logical Society as a metaphor for the new kind of approach to listening that he had in mind – he recalled, for example, that Nearing thought it was preferable to travel to and from the site in different ways so as to see different things; but, Cage added, even if one had to go the same way for both directions, one could still notice different things on the way back.[10]

Thus it was that Cage continued to attract his most enthusiastic audience from communities decidedly uninvolved with the classi-cal music scene: dancers, artists and writers, as well as people who loved the idea of creativity but were largely untrained: these flocked to Cage in droves. His message – that music is everywhere once you decide to pay attention to it – nurtured and inspired them.

As a composer, Cage was engaged in activity on several simul-taneous fronts, which included satisfying a substantial amount of interest in his earlier music for percussion and prepared piano. He acted as his own publishing company, furnishing copies of his music and even small kits of piano preparations. However, after writing the incidental music in 1960 for a Jackson Mac Low play, *The Marrying Maiden*, he became frustrated by the endless administrative duties required of a self-published com-poser and so refused to write another note until he had found professional representation.

After a few unsuccessful attempts, he contacted C. F. Peters, originally a German publisher that had been active throughout the nineteenth century. The Hinrichsen family, who had owned Peters since 1867, was committed to publishing the newest music in addition to maintaining the quality of its classical composers catalogue through new scholarship and editorial work. When Walter Hinrichsen (1907–1969) established the US office of Peters in New York, he continued the practice of publishing music by young composers. By 1962 the firm represented 58 American composers, and its associate, Henmar Press, another seventeen. Hinrichsen was delighted to hear from Cage; he told him that his wife had been urging him to publish Cage's music for some time. That very day, the two men had lunch and finalized a professional agreement that would continue until the end of Cage's life. Hinrichsen's decision to publish Cage with Henmar Press struck many as a controversial move, particularly in view of Cage's investment in such outré work as *4'33"*

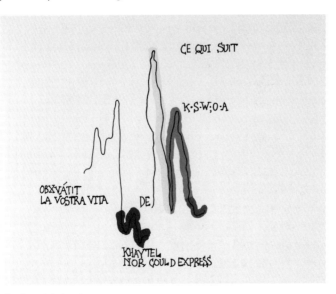

John Cage, *Aria* (1958), excerpt.

(1952) and *Radio Music* (1956), but it went a long way in further cementing his reputation.[11]

Cage's own newest musical activities clearly reflected his students' sense of pioneering by blurring the lines between music and theatre. An earlier period in Rome anticipated this development. There he associated with Luciano Berio and Berio's then wife, Cathy Berberian, which allowed him the opportunity to work with one of the greatest twentieth-century singers. For her he composed *Aria* (1958), a series of floating contours on twenty pages with a text in five languages selected by chance operations. The lines were of different types, in ten colours, two of which were additionally distinguished by parallel dotted lines; the singer was instructed to adopt distinct vocal styles for each. Berberian had already displayed a flair for the dramatic in Berio's electronic work *Thema (Omaggio a Joyce)*; soon afterward her husband would place that theatricality in a performance context with his *Circles*.

In Cage's *Theatre Piece* (1960) – very likely a response to his contact with the artists in his New School composition class – each performer's part contained numbers of different sizes, with or without xs. The large numbers correspond to 20 nouns and/or verbs selected by the performers as the basis for their actions. The cast for this odd spectacle included David Tudor, Merce Cunningham and Carolyn Brown; Don Butterfield, tuba; Frank Rehak, trombone; Arline Carmen, contralto; and Nicola Cernovich and Richard Nelson, two lighting designers who ended up not doing their job but instead spontaneously joined the other artists on stage. Brown recalled that she had tried to follow Cage's instructions as precisely as she could, though to her surprise he asked why she hadn't done more of a movement he'd liked. ('It only came up once', Brown replied.) The piece was panned by critics but amused the audience; Cage thought that, with the exception of Tudor, the performers had misunderstood his instructions.[12]

John Cage and David Tudor, *c.* 1960.

The year 1961 saw the premiere of *Where Are We Going? And What Are We Doing?*, a text composition that actually superimposes four separate lectures referring to music, Zen and Wittgenstein and thus more resembles the natural complexity of the universe that Cage so prized. The performance – by Cage with the other parts pre-recorded – obscured the boundaries separating lecture, poetry and music.

Other works from the early 1960s were explicit in their focus on sound, but their novelty and Cage's new vision of musical time made them equally challenging. In *Cartridge Music* (1960), tiny objects (pipe cleaners, feathers, matches) are placed into old-fashioned phonograph cartridges rather than the usual stylus; rubbing on or striking against the objects, amplified, allows the sounds they make to be heard.

At first, one hardly knows how to listen to such music; the electronics lend a certain harshness to the sounds that makes them seem overly mechanical. Soon enough, though, the complexity of the sounds becomes noticeable: the rubbed ones, for instance, have subtle rises or falls within a microscopic range of pitch, and the separate materials (metal, wood and so on) also have distinct and predictable timbres. In some cases the sounds are nearly inaudible; their combination with ambient sound seems to produce a timbre of its own. Depending on the fidelity of the performance (whether experienced only through a recording or in a concert), the different sounds eventually interact with each other in a delicate counterpoint. Those who hold with Cage's dictum that art imitates nature in her manner of operation will be reminded of all the tiny, complex rustlings heard outdoors, or perhaps the creaks and groans of an older house in the dead of night. The longer the performance, the more acutely the listener is confronted by these sensations. In Cage long durations are important in the experience: if the piece is too short, the noises cannot penetrate sufficiently to allow the experience of their interactions with each other and the environment.

If *Cartridge Music* created an opportunity for the exploration of extremely soft, ordinary sounds, *Atlas Eclipticalis* (1961–2) metaphorically extended that exploration to a universe of twinkling sounds separated by the vast expanse of silent space. For indeed Cage created the pitch material for this monumental orchestra piece by tracing the markings of stars from an astronomical map and adding staff lines that only partially clarified them: the staff lines are too large for the tiny noteheads, suggesting that the pitches they represent belong to a wider frequency range than can be accommodated by the Western musical scale.

When realized with a long total duration, the piece comes to resemble, not a performance of sounding music, but a visit to a large museum filled with artworks whose individualities all blend in with each other after a short while. And, as in a museum, one hardly imagines it possible to see and assimilate everything in one visit. Worse: since *Atlas* unfolds in time, one does not have the luxury of even choosing how much time to spend with a work, or the ability to return to something previously viewed. And because all the instrumental parts in *Atlas* can be performed singly or in any imaginable combination, the work can sound vastly different every time it is performed.

Other works, many conceived with Tudor in mind, stretched boundaries even further. In *Variations III* (1963) the performer must create the notation she performs from by tossing a number of circles printed on transparencies; each circle within the largest number of interlocking circles then corresponds to an action with as many aspects as the number of other circles with which it intersects. Or it may correspond to a number of separate actions equal to the number of intersections. Cage's opaque instructions allow for these and other possible interpretations. The performer begins with one circle and acts in accordance with the number of intersections; the performance, which can last any length of time, ends after repeating this process with each of the remaining circles.

Cage wrote that other performers could fulfil their roles by observing events occurring around them. As a final *coup de foudre*, he added this extraordinary instruction: 'Any other activities are going on at the same time.' In a single stroke, Cage included every other contingency, willed or unwilled, as part of his music. Any action that could produce a sound – a cough, breath, rustling in a chair – contributed to the work.

Cage's fame was established less by these extraordinarily confounding works than by his first published book, *Silence*, which made his ideas widely accessible to the public. It appeared in 1961 at the close of a one-year academic fellowship at Wesleyan University, whose press issued it. Fifty years later, *Silence* continues to be both provocative and highly entertaining.

The essays come from a long period in Cage's life, ranging from the late 1930s to 1961. As such, it collapses and obscures the long trajectory of Cage's work from his first enthusiasm with sounds of all sorts, to his methods of structuring them, and ultimately to his discovery of sources for his later work, above all Indian aesthetics and Zen Buddhism. To be sure, some of the content of *Silence* is highly technical: severe, concise and almost painful descriptions of Cage's chance composition unleavened by any personality whatever. But probably *Silence* is particularly beloved for the witty stories of 'Indeterminacy' (1958–9), scattered here and there like little Easter eggs of poetic whimsy. Cage certainly knew how to tell a funny story:

> When Vera Williams first noticed that I was interested in wild mushrooms, she told her children not to touch any of them because they were all deadly poisonous. A few days later she bought a steak at Martino's and decided to serve it smothered with mushrooms. When she started to cook the mushrooms, the children all stopped what they were doing and watched her attentively. When she served dinner, they all burst into tears.[13]

But other passages are quite different and presented, moreover, in a very novel way. As mentioned in chapter Three, 'Composition as Process: Communication' comprises a striking series of unanswered questions occasionally relieved by quotations from Christian Wolff, Zhuangzi and others. In one unforgettable passage, Cage argues for an expanded sense of art.

> If words are sounds, are they musical or are they just noises?
> If sounds are noises but not words, are they meaningful?

Are they musical?

Say there are two sounds and two people and one of each is
   beautiful, is there between all four any communication?

And if there are rules, who made them, I ask you?

Does it begin somewhere, I mean, and if so, where does it stop?

What will happen to me or to you if we have to be somewhere
   where beauty isn't?

I ask you, sometime, too, sounds happening in time, what will
   happen to our experience of hearing, yours, mine, our ears,
   hearing, what will happen if sounds being beautiful stop
   sometime and the only sounds to hear are not beautiful to
   hear but are ugly, what will happen to us?

Would we ever be able to get so that we thought the ugly sounds
   were beautiful?[14]

Other writings reflect Zen by example. The *45' for a Speaker*
(1954), while it cobbles together quotations from earlier Cage
texts, makes frequent reference to Zen and D. T. Suzuki. But
as a mosaic of unrelated or loosely related remarks, it seems to
embody the principles of unimpededness and interpenetration
that he attributed to Suzuki. Indeed, the 'Indeterminacy' stories
extend this metaphor to include the relevance of many things
completely unrelated to music at all (observations of daily life,
family anecdotes and so on).

   In short, a reader of *Silence* generally did not need to have
any kind of professional training to enjoy the book – and to be
profoundly affected by it. How different this was from the main
American mouthpiece of professional new music composition,
Perspectives of New Music. Here, Babbitt, his colleagues and younger
protégés eagerly discussed the latest trends in music in great detail;
its methodological approach required an extreme level of professional training to understand – in particular, the analysis of the
new music borrowed principles from mathematics to model the

music analysed: Boulez's idea of research, dreamt of but never really carried out by him, had in fact been realized by the *Perspectives* cadre. And while it led and continues to lead composers towards new and robust modes of expression, a casual spectator of *Perspectives* would react to it just as Babbitt predicted the hordes of unlettered cretins in 'Who Cares if You Listen?' would react when confronted with these new ideas – they would hate it and have no way to understand it.

Truth to tell, the hordes of the unlettered probably never *did* have much of a chance to react to *Perspectives* one way or another. The journal was available chiefly through subscription, and its contents were discussed in classrooms, conferences and its own pages – not in the newspapers or popular magazines that had, from time to time, covered Cage's singular brand of bohemian avant-gardism.

Silence occasioned considerable critical debate. Jill Johnston, dance critic for the *Village Voice*, commented favourably on the agreeable variety of material. While her description of Cage's compositional methods was too cursory to give a full impression of them, her understanding of Cage's critique of conventional aesthetics was extremely perceptive. She stressed the importance of experience over judgement in audition; she acknowledged the advantage of multiple responses to the music; and she suggested that Cage's conception of art returned humanity to a position within nature rather than one that dominated it. In particular, she astutely recognized that the ambient sound immanent within what was conventionally understood as silence should be understood as a cosmic complement to whatever sounds Cage added. (Its presence as such, of course, was already alerted by *4'33"*.) Perhaps she was overly confident when she imagined the experiencing subject as 'empty of memories, ideas, and preconceptions'.[15]

Perspectives of New Music published its own review of *Silence* in due course, by the poet John Hollander; his review indicated what worried the mainstream professional musical establishment about

Cage's work. Hollander systematically undermined Cage's works by referring to them as *productions* – implying at once the anonymity of the factory-made commodity and the garish display of mass media entertainment. With that representation in place, Hollander critiqued the success of the works as commodity and spectacle. Referring to a late-night performance of *Imaginary Landscape No. 4* (1951), a work for twelve radios, he remarked that the piece should have been performed earlier in the evening (so as to capture more varied sounds) and been shorter (probably so that its primary function as a joke could not overstay its welcome). Hollander felt that Cage's abdication of his own authority as composer released the listener from any obligation to take his music seriously and listen carefully. Worse, it implied that Cage's chosen methods could never allow for the process of critical reflection and hard work that characterizes real art and real artists.[16]

In spite of the differing conclusions made by both reviewers, each suffered from a common problem, the omission of one crucial phenomenon from their commentary: the actual *sounds* of Cage's music. Johnston gushed that he rescued music from setting itself apart from life, rescued it from the tyranny of composers who wanted to bludgeon listeners into hearing certain things and feeling certain things. Now listeners were free to make their own experiences of the music. But she never shared her experiences; and Hollander sidestepped the question altogether by asserting that the music was more enjoyable to read about than experience.

Meanwhile, Cage's flair for polemic continued by way of increasing attention on Erik Satie. His fascination with the French composer dated from the late 1940s, when he had first argued that Satie's musical structures were primarily rhythmic, not harmonic, and thus representative of the true course for the future of music. In the 1950s, as Cage moved towards chance and indeterminacy, Satie became something else for him: yet another authority figure that justified all of his latest preoccupations. Cage chided the music critic Abraham Skulsky for claiming that Satie used humour to mask the deficiencies in his art, and that Satie was influential but not great himself. By contrast, Cage argued, Satie was important precisely because he was indifferent to the expectations for art to be lofty or impressive – like a Zen master, Satie remained unattached to any motives for music, and thus could laugh or cry as he chose.[17] No doubt Cage also appreciated Satie's idea of *musique d'ameublement* (furniture music) that ceased to be concert music and rather functioned only as a utility with which to experience everyday life.

Perhaps, too, Cage projected a certain anxiety he felt that, as his pieces became more radical, critics no longer felt his own music was worthwhile: that younger associates like Morton Feldman, Earle Brown, Wolff and Boulez would be seen as the important composers while Cage himself was best known for his forward-thinking ideas. This view is indeed one that began to appear around this time and continues to this day.

Cage remained inspired by Satie for the rest of his life, and in September 1963 his wonder for the French composer touched a whole group of younger artists. In 1893 Satie wrote a curious piece without bar lines: an oddly melodic bass of thirteen quavers, the same bass with two harmonizing treble lines, and the bass with the higher of the treble lines moved to the middle of the texture; he insisted that this piece, called *Vexations*, should be executed 840 times in succession, thereby affording its performer the possibility of achieving 'inward mobility'. The music itself is neither tonal nor atonal – its ambiguous but only mildly dissonant harmonies suggest the possibility of going somewhere, but listeners never can be sure where. The piece contains needlessly confusing notation that constantly disorients performers – and these vagaries only increase through multiple repetitions of the music.

Previously no one had dared to take Satie's instructions literally, but rather had interpreted them in the same manner as the numerous odd performance indications to be found in his scores – remarks like 'play like a nightingale with a toothache' or to play as 'light as an egg'. But Cage decided to take Satie at his word and engineer at New York's Pocket Theater a performance of *Vexations* to include each and every one of those 840 iterations. In all twelve pianists participated, including Tudor, Wolff and the composer James Tenney. As Cage later observed, the experience had results that no one could foresee: the very act of continuous performance created a new space for the experience of art: the aimless noodling both tranquillized and transfigured the players and the audience so as to create an alternative mode of attention that was neither wakefulness nor repose, but perhaps something closer to consciously experiencing the normal pace of everyday time, everyday life. Wolff recalled in 1974:

> As the first cycle of pianists went round the playing was quite diverse, a variety – quite extreme, from the most sober and cautious to the willful and effusive – of personalities was revealed. Musically the effect seemed disturbing. But after another round the more expansive players began to subside, the more restrained to relax, and by the third round or so the personalities and playing techniques of the pianists had been almost completely subsumed by the music. The music simply took over. At first a kind of passive object, it became the guiding force. . . . As the night wore on we got weary, or rather just sleepy, and the beautiful state of suspension of self now became risky. Alertness had to be redoubled not to miss repetitions or notes. An element of comedy – now that solidarity and easiness were evidently there – joined us.[18]

In spite of Cage's prodigious activities as a composer and writer, his primary occupation was that of music director – as well as chauffeur, cook and overall cheerleader – for the Merce Cunningham Dance Company. His work with them had already begun to accelerate by

Merce Cunningham in performance, *c.* 1965.

the mid-1950s, when he and Merce borrowed money for a Volks-
wagen bus just large enough to accommodate the dancers – including
Carolyn Brown, Remy Charlip and Viola Farber – along with Cage,
Cunningham, Tudor, Cernovich and costumes.[19]

Cunningham's presence was inspiring but also unfathomable.
Like Cage he wanted to liberate movement from the standard
conventions of the dance – not only by enlarging the repertory of
movement itself, but also by increasing the number of simultaneous
movements by a single dancer. As Cunningham moved, it seemed as
if all his limbs were independent of his torso and could move in all
sorts of directions, seemingly of their own volition.

With his company, Cunningham sought not to impose his will on
the dancers when he made works, but rather help them to discover
how his movements needed to be executed through their own bodies
and their individual characteristics. His dance phrases did not depend
on music, and if he based them on other poetic stimulus, he rarely
shared this inspiration with anyone else. His movement, rather,
was shaped and perfected with respect to time: stopwatch in hand,
Cunningham carefully refined his phrases until he discovered the
ideal time they took to perform. Thereafter he would train the dancers
to match that ideal as closely as possible. Without music or other
obvious cues, the dancers had to depend largely on muscle memory
alone. Frequently he had to show the movements as they would occur
in real time; to slow them down would subtly alter the fluidity of
muscle motion needed to execute them correctly.

Cunningham's reluctance to impose his will on others also meant
that he was less than forthcoming either with praise or blame.
Carolyn Brown remembered that Charlip, who was losing his hair,
found out secondhand that Cunningham wanted him to wear a
toupee. And Brown agonized to please him, often without ever
knowing whether she did or not.

Yet in spite of this the close-knit quarters of the vw bus created a
sense of community within the company. Cage, who (recalling Black

Mountain) once sagely observed that community can be created simply by eating together, memorialized his years with the company with a text including descriptions of some unforgettable meals he shared with them:

> We descended like a plague of locusts
> on the Brownsville Eat-All-You-Want
> Restaurant ($1.50). Just for dessert
> Steve Paxton had five pieces of pie. Merce
> asked cashier: How do you manage to keep
> this place going? 'Most people', she
> replied rather sadly, 'don't eat as much
> as you people.'[20]

During those days Cage also insisted on having happy hour promptly at five every afternoon.

Although Cunningham performed frequently in the US, it was in Europe that the company would enjoy its greatest early successes. At the XXIII Festival Internazionale di Musica Contemporanea, a performance in Venice's famed Teatro La Fenice on 24 September 1960 divided the audience pro and con. Stravinsky, who actually attended the performance, wryly assured journalists that Cunningham's riot was not as spectacular as the one occasioned by his own *Rite*. Later on, in Cologne, the company was treated to a harrowing and darkly comic performance by the Korean avant-garde artist Nam June Paik, who destroyed two pianos, cut off Cage's tie with scissors, lathered Cage's and Tudor's heads with shampoo, and eventually ran from the studio with a dead mouse clenched between his teeth. A few minutes later, he called to say that the performance, *Étude for Pianoforte*, was over.[21]

Back in America, Cage became convinced that Cunningham needed to do a series of shows on Broadway to advance the company's reputation. Money was raised by selling artworks donated by a who's who in American art including Robert Rauschenberg, Jasper Johns, Robert Motherwell and Andy Warhol. But a writer's strike precluded the possibility of generating the desired amount of press and so delayed the show; trips to the West Coast pushed the date back further. In the end, it was decided to raise more money and undertake a world tour instead. Cage raised a considerable sum by selling a wire sculpture by Richard Lippold. In July the company boarded an Air France flight to Paris.

Rauschenberg, who had joined the company as lighting designer, also generously helped keep the company solvent. The company scored a particular triumph in London, where they performed for a total of four weeks. By contrast, Cage's music had little critical impact and was sometimes roundly criticized. It seemed clear that this was a time for Cunningham and his company, especially Carolyn Brown, who by now demanded top billing.

Meanwhile, public attention paid to Rauschenberg began to vie for Cunningham's acclaim, and perhaps to surpass it. For Rauschenberg was the prizewinner in painting at the 1964 Venice Biennale, and was now followed by a coterie of admirers. No doubt Cage's great love for Cunningham made it harder for him to bear this turn of events. Brown recalled that the adoration for the artist annoyed Cage, who told Rauschenberg, 'There can only be one star here!'[22] Rauschenberg responded by finding the company's financial manager, Lewis Lloyd, and demanding that a $1,000 loan be repaid.

The arduous schedule of performances took its toll mentally and physically. In India, Cage's music was vilified. In Tokyo, Rauschenberg was feted by the press. A misunderstanding, fuelled by earlier tensions, made Rauschenberg believe that Cage and Cunningham deliberately attended an event in Rauschenberg's honour for only a few minutes; the angry artist resigned with obvious hurt feelings. And he was not alone. Cunningham had lost one dancer in London, and four more members resigned along with Rauschenberg at the end of the tour.

After returning from Europe, Cage began to intensify his interest in technology in the creation of art. For years he had written to potential benefactors to fund a centre for experimental music, especially using electronics. Babbitt and others had succeeded in establishing one of the first electronic music studios (which were also just as often called laboratories – extensions of Babbitt's R&D model of composition); the one at Princeton sported a unique music synthesizer, the RCA Mark II.

Cage now sought support from Bell Laboratories; with the help of Bell employees Tenney and Max Mathews, and assisted by Robert Moog (who had recently unveiled his eponymous synthesizer, which was about to revolutionize electronic music) and the physicist Billy Klüver, they worked together to produce an elaborate network of gadgetry – motion-activated sensors that triggered an array of radios and tape recorders – that could be used in the creation of yet another collaboration with Cunningham. *Variations v*, first performed at Lincoln Center on 23 July 1965, marked the first of several large-scale works involving dance, music and substantive technology.

It was not Cage's first foray into this arena. He had already worked with Mathews (and with the funding of Bell Labs) to produce a 50-channel mixer that Cage used in a disastrous performance of *Atlas Eclipticalis* by the New York Philharmonic conducted by Bernstein on 6–9 February 1964. Cage had equipped the musicians with inexpensive contact microphones, which would route the sounds into a mixer whose output was controlled by Cage and Tenney; thus, the musicians knew that there was no guarantee their work would even be heard. In their frustration with this seemingly arbitrary caprice, the musicians revolted. They removed the microphones and stamped on them, which made it necessary for Cage to purchase replacements; they played whatever they felt like playing (just as the musicians premiering the 1958 *Concert for Piano and Orchestra*). Years later, he remembered the humiliating experience:

The New York Philharmonic is a bad orchestra. They're like a group of gangsters. They have no shame: When I came off the stage after one of those performances, one of them who had played badly shook my hand, smiled, and said, 'Come back in ten years, we'll treat you better.' They turn things away from music, and from any professional attitude toward music, to some kind of social situation that is not very beautiful.[23]

Another work involving technology was more modest but more evocative: *Rozart Mix* (1965), originally performed in the Rose Art Museum at Brandeis University in Waltham, Massachusetts. The score for this work consists entirely of correspondence between Cage and Alvin Lucier, the composer who invited Cage to the event and who, with Cage's encouragement, presented at the same concert his pioneering *Music for Solo Performer*, the sound material of which is derived from his own amplified brainwaves.

Rose Art Museum, Brandeis University.

To realize *Rozart Mix*, the performers construct 88 tape loops, which are played on a number of tape recorders; the loops, of various sizes, could be as long as the length of the museum space. Lucier recalled that the splicing instructions were guaranteed to produce extremely unusual sounds:

> As we were going about our simple tasks of threading, replacing and occasionally repairing our loops, we could sometimes recognize loops that we had made, but more often than not, the mix of sounds in the Museum was overwhelming. In those parts of loops which were spliced with tiny fragments of tape, no sound was identifiable. Those made up of longer segments – none were supposed to be more than four or five inches long – gave the impression of collage.[24]

As in many other works of this decade, Cage would not end the piece until most of the audience had left the museum.

Variations v proved to be far more elaborate; the dancers triggered the sensors, which, in turn, activated circuitry in the mixer to route a variety of sound material on tapes and radios through a multichannel speaker system. In addition the mixer's output would be adjusted, and some of the dancers and props were also equipped with contact microphones that amplified their actions. But the interactions of these elements were such that no one person was responsible for the sounds that were actually heard.

The sound was deafening; the myriad devices had not been tested until the only rehearsal in the hall and probably did not operate as they had been intended to. But the results, while not ideal, were successful enough.[25] Unbelievably, *Variations v* toured the US and Europe over two years, and Cage embarked on a series of other similar events involving technology. *Variations vii* (1966), for instance, was part of the category-breaking Nine Evenings: Experiments in Art and Technology, which involved artists and Bell Lab engineers.

John Cage and Merce Cunningham, *Variations v* (1965): Cage, David Tudor and Gordon Mumma (foreground); Carolyn Brown, Cunningham and Barbara Dilley (background); film by Stan VanDerBeek; TV images by Nam June Paik.

By the late 1960s Cage abdicated his position as the company's music director and, while he continued to perform with them, began ever more frequent travel as a guest artist and in a series of residencies at American universities. At the University of Illinois, he arrived at a method to create a practical and edifying liberation of performers with his activity to assemble the premiere perform-ance of his *Musicircus* (1968). The musicians participating in this event could perform any music they wished – any style, for any instrumentation and at any volume. So long as many musicians were involved, and so long as they remained in one large space, Cage felt that the sound they produced would be so complex and heterogeneous that it could in effect erase the sense of any single personality, even if a musician chose to act as comically as some did in the *Concert* and *Atlas*. Multiplicity and abundance brought about the ennobling freedom that Cage sought through his art. Although *Musicircus* was a successful event, the intense freedoms Cage permitted during its performance posed real dangers for the audience. The noise level exceeded the threshold of safety several times and, in one notable moment, Cage further encouraged a sense of pandemonium by arbitrarily switching the lights on and off.[26]

In the other major project of Cage's Illinois residency, he fulfilled a long-standing request from the Swiss harpsichordist Antoinette Vischer for a new work. After much delay, owing to Cage's dislike of the harpsichord's sound, he decided to fulfil the commission by adding to it the sound of electronically generated pitches in a variety of tunings. The composer Lejaren Hiller had promised Cage a computer programmer to assist in the vast amount of programming needed to bring the piece into existence (which included computerizing the I Ching itself); but the assistant turned out to be unavailable, and Hiller took over the work himself. Cage eventually suggested that Hiller name himself as the co-composer of the piece.

The figurational variety in Mozart's music was taken as a model. Indeed, one of the eventual seven harpsichord solos consisted solely of music generated by Mozart's *Musical Dice Game* (K294d), while another simply required the performer to perform or practise any work of Mozart.

The resulting work, *HPSCHD* (the title renders the word 'harpsichord' in six letters, the limit for titles of computer files at the time), was presented in a large open space in a mammoth performance lasting five hours on 16 May 1969. Commemorative t-shirts were available, and the audience members who wandered in the round were also treated to all manner of visual stimulus provided by the artists Ron Nameth and Calvin Sumsion. Of all Cage's pieces this one was one of the most joyous, with the constant, buoyant triple metre of the Mozart dice game solo ever present alongside many other sounds of every possible description. Here the constant activity seems akin to some perverse avant-garde circus – Cage's clearest idea of a happening.[27]

The premiere of *HPSCHD*, 16 May 1969, Assembly Hall, University of Illinois, Urbana.

Cage's rise in the 1960s came at a propitious moment. The US had begun its most tumultuous decade. A number of factors that arose coincidentally formed the synergy for this smouldering decade of discord: the conservative conformity of the 1950s was undermined by an increasingly young population who resisted dominant methods of polity in increasing numbers, from students demanding freedom of speech at the University of California, Berkeley, in 1964 to vast experimentation with sex, drugs and rock 'n' roll by 1968 and 1969. America's growing sense of itself as a conglomeration of different cultures distinguished by ethnicity, gender or sexual preference led to wide-ranging and sustained demands to be treated with dignity and equality. A long, painful war in Vietnam helped to unite these disparate groups into a more general call that shook America's foundations as a world power whose every action was justified.

Much of this sentiment resonated with Cage's own sense of aesthetics and politics. His own desire to liberate sounds from the composer's authority was a non-violent revolt in support for sonic civil rights. Implicit in his critique was the notion that the institutionalized avant-garde ensconced in academia only pretended to be a progressive force and was allied with the European worldview, which Cage had already experienced first-hand in Donaueschingen and Darmstadt. His increasing embrace of the non-academic wing of the musical establishment led him to adopt a tone of naive wisdom that was as eloquent as it was subversive. The experimental attitude he explored throughout the decade would overlap the spirit of unbridled curiosity for the new. And as radicals of all ages asserted their individuality in dress, music and dissidence, so Cage's eternal faith in and regard for the individual increased.

But there were also important differences. Most importantly, Cage was wary of any assertions of group power, which could coerce the weak-minded and timid into having beliefs they had not decided to adopt through their own critical thought. And what Cage feared was exactly what happened. Criminals – above all, drug dealers – cashed in as, for some, experimentation degraded into addiction; and sociopaths like Charles Manson used charisma to prey upon disenfranchised women and lead them into acts of cruelty and violence. As the era of Kennedy and Johnson ended with the election of Nixon and the nascent emergence of a neoconservatism, increasing shows of force were marshalled to quell student riots and any other signs of dissent.

The political fervour of the time began to subside even as blacks, Latinos, gays and women began to gain increasing equality. By the time the war ended in 1973 Americans had become increasingly disenchanted with government and concomitantly paralysed by the malaise of indifference. And Cage, whose popularity had reached its zenith with *HPSCHD*, would soon make his greatest music.

5

Doyen

During the years leading up to Cage's 60th birthday in 1972, thoughts of mortality coloured his work and his famously optimistic disposition. In October 1968 Marcel Duchamp died; Duchamp had become for Cage, if not one of his legendary figures of authority, a friend of singular importance. He had asked the older artist to teach him chess in order to have a pretext for spending time with him; in the process, Cage learned a great deal about the game, but his playful approach towards it annoyed Duchamp, who once, exasperated, asked, 'Don't you ever want to win?'[1]

They had last seen each other in Toronto the previous March. There, he and Cage participated in a work Cage made called *Reunion*, during which they played chess on a board equipped (by Lowell Cross) with 64 photoresistors. When the photoresistors passed a signal as the chess pieces were moved, electronic or electroacoustic music created by four composers – Gordon Mumma, David Behrman, David Tudor and Cross himself – would be routed to speakers positioned around the audience. The first game ended in less than half an hour (Cage lost); in the second, which lasted until one o'clock the next morning, Cage played Duchamp's wife, Teeny, while the master looked on.[2]

Sadly, Cage's mother also died in the same month and year as Duchamp. Since the time his father had died in 1964, Crete had resided in an assisted living community. A few stories about her appear in Cage's mosaic-like diary – really a text composition much

Performing *Reunion* in Toronto, 1968: Teeny Duchamp, Marcel Duchamp, John Cage.

like the various stories of *Indeterminacy* – that he began writing in 1965: 'I noticed the nurses were kind to her. "Naturally they are. If you like people, people like you."'[3] Its full title, *Diary: How to Improve the World (You Can Only Make Matters Worse)*, gave yet another sense of the self-reflexive, ironic attitude with which Cage leavened his customary optimism. In the *Diary* and elsewhere, too, he began to record medical problems of various sorts, from a sty (which one eye-doctor misdiagnosed) to arthritis that left his wrists misshapen and obliged him to take many aspirin a day; he even went so far as to observe, in 1973, that he was on his 'last legs'.[4]

His old age resulted in other decisions as well. In September 1970 he began living with Cunningham at the latter's apartment in New York, on Bank Street in Greenwich Village. (For a time John Lennon and Yoko Ono were his neighbours.) Although he continued to keep his other dwelling in Stony Point, he now complained about the general atmosphere of the place, comparing it to a 'shanty town'; he also confessed that he was afraid of falling on the ice in wintertime. David Nicholls hypothesizes that Cage's return to New York might have derived from a quasi-Freudian motive: now that both parents – who had lived close to New York City – were dead, Cage no longer needed to create distance between himself and them.[5] Of course, for Cage, home was something of an illusion in any case, because his growing fame had led to near-constant travel all over the world.

Perhaps the changing political landscape in the late 1960s and '70s also played a role in Cage's darker mood. The 1960s were over and with them the sense of limitless abandon that had seemed possible. In America the change began in 1969, with the presidential inauguration of Richard Nixon. Nixon was a brilliant statesman, but his conservatism guaranteed that the US did not continue along the lines of vigorous dissent that had previously characterized the country. What is more, Nixon promised that the American presence in Vietnam would end, but would do so without any loss of dignity. And it seemed, too, that the American people had tired of protest and social upheaval. The great social experiment of the hippies, already marred by Charles Manson, now suffered new attacks as scrutiny of their favoured doors of perception – hallucinogenic drugs – intensified. Some artists of that time paid dearly for their excesses, including Janis Joplin, Jimi Hendrix and Jim Morrison: all three had died before the age of 30. America was tired of death, so Nixon's message of hope and a restoration to normalcy appealed to many.

Nevertheless, the promised peace in Vietnam proved all too elusive. Secret negotiations – conducted in October 1972 by Nixon's secretary of state, Henry Kissinger, with the North Vietnamese president – led to the premature announcement of peace; when the negotiations became stalled, Nixon enforced the deal through the horrific Christmas bombing of Hanoi. The American withdrawal began in 1973. So too began televised broadcasts of the so-called Watergate Hearings, which led eventually to a vote to impeach Nixon and, soon after, his ignominious resignation in August 1974. Cage confessed that, like millions of other Americans, he watched the broadcasts utterly transfixed, in a state of dumbfounded gloom; elsewhere he called it the longest Happening America had ever experienced, comparable to Greek or Nōh drama.[6]

The political situation in America must have strengthened Cage's resolve to pursue an ideology that many have labelled as utopianism, but which Cage himself always referred to as anarchism. He named himself as an anarchist as early as 1961, in the foreword to *Silence*, but he never explained fully what he meant by the appellation. Not so much a doctrine as it is an ensemble of contingent beliefs, anarchism lacks a strong theoretical base, lacks even consensus regarding many of its defining characteristics. Cage was familiar, in particular, with the work of the American anarchists; he approvingly referred several times to James Martin's history of American anarchism published in 1953, as well as to the work of Emma Goldman.[7] For Cage, anarchism probably meant not so much its familiar meaning of a state of chaotic and dangerous lawlessness, but rather something closer to a definition written by Peter Kropotkin, the Russian anarchist who authored a widely acclaimed article on the subject for the eleventh edition of *Encyclopædia Britannica*. Kropotkin maintained that anarchism involved 'a principle or theory of life and conduct under which society is conceived without government', where harmony arises through 'free agreements concluded between the various groups'. Cage felt that any form of polity was coercive; as he expressed it to Daniel Charles, 'Politics consists of affirming and wanting domination.'[8]

Cage's anarchistic project also encompassed such countercultural ideas as the liberation of utilities to be made useful for all people, a global concern for ecology and the abolishment of nations to be replaced by shared intelligence and technological resources for the solution of world problems. These ideas, in turn, exemplify his considerable debt to two of his favourite twentieth-century thinkers, Buckminster Fuller and Marshall McLuhan, whom – along with many others – Cage cites in the *Diary*'s pages.

Although he knew and loved the writings of many anarchists, including the violent Mikhail Bakunin, the man Cage singled out most often in connection with his social beliefs was another American, Henry David Thoreau. He had first encountered Thoreau's work through the poet Wendell Berry, whom he met in 1967 during a question and answer session following a performance of the Merce Cunningham Dance Company in Kentucky. At a later meeting in Berry's home, the poet read aloud from Thoreau's eleven-volume *Journal*, and Cage instantly knew that he needed to become acquainted with it. By reading Thoreau himself, Cage acknowledged that he discovered 'any idea I've ever had worth its salt'.[9] From that point onward, Thoreau joined Schoenberg, Suzuki and Satie in his personal pantheon of inspirational authorities. One cryptic remark in the *Diary*, 'We connect Satie with Thoreau', became clear to him only later, with the making of his *Song Books* (1970);[10] and Thoreau's *Journal* served as the source for one of Cage's most important text compositions, *Empty Words* (1973–4), both of which are discussed further below.[11]

Although Cage remained faithful to the ideas of flux and the unexpected, two important compositions he made in 1969 and 1970 called into question many of the fundamental assumptions about his work.

In 1945 Merce Cunningham had begun a choreography to the first movement of Erik Satie's *Socrate*, a kind of monodrama for soprano and orchestra with a text taken from the dialogues of Plato documenting the end of Socrates' life; now Cunningham hoped to finish it with the remaining movements. Cage had arranged the first of the work's three movements for two pianos and, in 1969, undertook the arrangement's completion. Unfortunately, Satie's publishers forbade its performance.

Cage was at a crossroads; there was no possibility of substituting other music: Cunningham's choreography was carefully wedded to

John Cage rehearsing with Merce Cunningham Dance Company at Westbeth, New York City, 1972.

the phrasing and ethos of the Satie. (When he had made the first movement, he had not yet reached the point in his work where he was willing wholly to liberate the dance from music.) Cage's solution, characteristically, combined ingenuity and mirthful goodwill: he retained the rhythms of Satie's music, but through chance operations altered the pitches entirely: a single melodic line remained – scored for solo piano – that originally belonged to the voice in Satie's music or, when the voice was silent, to the orchestra. Often enough, as in the beginning of the last movement, sufficient vestiges of Satie's original music remain, linking the new music to the old with the affinity of familial resemblance. Cage called the piece *Cheap Imitation*; Cunningham renamed his dance *Second Hand*.

Initially Cage found it difficult to reconcile this work with the aesthetic project to which he had devoted himself. Throughout the 1960s he had increasingly spoken against musical objects – fixed compositions that sounded the same every time they were performed – in favour of processes that performers had to realize themselves and, sometimes, that even allowed the unfolding process of realization to form the material seen and heard by the audience. In Cage's first performance of *Variations III* (1963), for instance, one of his actions was to drink with amplification at such a high level that 'each swallow reverberated through the hall like the pounding of a giant surf.'[12]

Cheap Imitation, by contrast, was a musical object, not a process. It contained three movements and conventional rhythms. Furthermore, Cage's chance operations had rarely changed the pitches sufficiently to give them the disjointed, atomized character of so many of his other works. And, while Satie's music was hardly dramatic, it followed a certain trajectory that listeners found familiar; it did not resemble Cage's preferred processes.

Ever willing to change his mind, he embraced this difficulty and examined it carefully. Thereafter he did not reject the procedure he had discovered through necessity, but instead incorporated it into his subsequent work. In any event the utility of the *Cheap Imitation* technique became immediately apparent in his next major commission, *Song Books*, first performed in Paris in 1970. Cage conceived this monumental composition as a kind of summation of his work, perhaps in keeping with the thoughts of mortality that had occupied his mind since the death of his mother and Duchamp. It comprised 78 solo pieces involving theatre and song singly or in combination; cryptically, he considered each solo relevant or irrelevant to the mysterious remark from the *Diary*, 'We connect Satie with Thoreau'.

Song, for Cage, meant a wide range of possibilities: Solo 49, 'The Year begins to be ripe', reprises the music of the 1941 song *The Wonderful Widow of Eighteen Springs* with a new text, while Solo 58 comprises eighteen microtonal ragas. In Solo 3 the performer uses a map of Thoreau's beloved Concord, Massachusetts, to trace a prescribed path and then convert the drawing into a vocal line; in keeping with Cage's commitment to process, the singer needed to create the music she would perform. Still other solos recalled the

Amelia Cuni performing *Song Books*, Solo 58 (18 Microtonal Ragas), Venice Biennale, October 2007 (originally produced by MaerzMusik/ Berliner Festspiele).

complicated coordination of numbers with words that characterized *Theatre Piece*, and several literally repeated one of Cage's most unusual works, *0'00''* (1963), in which a performer undertakes any non-musical actions that fulfil a social obligation to others, actions that are amplified to the highest degree before distortion occurs. That Cage allowed any number of performers to fashion a programme of any agreed-upon length with any number of resulting superimpositions of material did not entirely negate the presence of musical numbers in *Song Books* that were clearly intended as *coups de théâtre*: one was an extraordinary adaptation of Mozart's aria for the Queen of the Night from Act Two of *Die Zauberflöte*.

Another specified element of *Song Books* indicated something else: at various points in the performance, one solo was to be sung in the manner of a recurring refrain: a series of settings of Thoreau's text, 'The best form of government is no government at all. / And that will be what men will have when they are ready for it.' These refrains, which were always to be accompanied by raising the black flag of anarchy or otherwise displaying the Circle-A symbol, were optimistic, in a foursquare metre – they sounded like the simple music appropriate for performance at a political rally.

As with *Cheap Imitation* before it, Cage seemed ambivalent about *Song Books*. During a public interview following its premiere, as he averred to an audience member, 'But at the present time to consider the *Song Books* as a work of art is nearly impossible. Who would dare? It resembles a brothel, doesn't it?' (*Laughter.*) [13] As time went on, however, he became ever more attracted to the work. In the crowning pieces of the previous decade – *Musicircus* (1968) and *HPSCHD* (1969) – Cage felt he had found a way to allow people to experience productive anarchism, whether they wanted to or not. Both works allowed a multiplicity of music to occur simultaneously; indeed, in *Musicircus* the participants could perform anything they wished. The superimposition of sound would free the performances from any intention whatsoever and allow everyone to experience that multiplicity together in spite of their own agency within it. The heterogeneity of *Song Books*, as well as the presence of the 'Best Form of Government' refrain, focused the work's political aim, making it both more elegant and incisive.

Cage's advancing age and fame helped increase enthusiasm for his work. Often, of course, that interest resulted in endless performances of his 1940s works for percussion and prepared piano – they were, after all, extremely attractive works that still retained traces of their iconoclastic spirit. Fortunately, other performers requested new works. The commissions of the 1970s following *Song Books* allowed Cage to explore, in a thoroughgoing manner, the political or social metaphors in his music – or, in his own words, to create art available for use in society. [14] His new pieces performed this cultural work through the development of two basic tropes: the celebration of individual autonomy – resulting in several brilliant solo compositions – or the forging of novel relationships among larger groups.

As always, Cage had very good results with soloists. For Grete Sultan, whom he had met years earlier through Richard Buhlig, Cage made the *Etudes Australes* (1974–5), initially from a desire to spare her the extreme violence of his *Music of Changes* (1951). Working once more from star charts, Cage traced a certain number according to chance; then, for each one, he determined whether the traced note would stand on its own or whether it would include other tones. If others were to be added, Cage made a selection from a catalogue of possible chords including one to four additional notes which could be performed comfortably by one hand; the likelihood that additional tones appeared tended to increase in the later etudes. Cage created additional sound by allowing certain bass strings – different ones in each etude – to vibrate freely so that a sheen of sympathetic resonance coloured the other tones.

Likewise, the violinist Paul Zukofsky also approached Cage about the possibility of new works, but made clear his wish to perform music with precise notation. As a virtuoso Zukofsky delighted in being offered technical challenges that he could then surmount. Cage responded with the series of *Freeman Etudes* (1977–80; 1989–90), commissioned for Zukofsky by the great American patron Betty Freeman. With the violinist, Cage compiled a catalogue of every possible combination of sounds the instrument could produce. These he used in conjunction with his technique of tracings from star maps to create a highly detailed and specific kind of piece that was resolutely modernistic, fiendishly difficult and – naturally – unlike anything that had been heard before.

But these extraordinary pieces also fulfilled Cage's wishes to produce useful music – in other words, to create music that could transcend its status as an artwork and point towards the ethical conduct of humanity in everyday life. The etudes were written, he said, in acknowledgement of the seeming powerlessness of the individual in the face of tremendous difficulties in the world. By extension, Cage imagined the idea of virtuosity not merely as the demonstration of extreme technical skill, not merely as an object to excite admiration, love and mystification:

> [The *Freeman Etudes*] are intentionally as difficult as I can make them, because I think we're now surrounded by very serious problems in the society, and we tend to think that the situation is hopeless and that it's just impossible to do something that will make everything turn out properly. So I think that this music, which is almost impossible, gives an instance of the practicality of the impossible.[15]

This quotation indicates Cage's unshakable belief that the individual could, through a process of self-discovery, effect the change of mindset that would transform life on earth.

A closer examination of the *Etudes Australes* reveals the degree to which Cage inscribed these social principles in the sound and sight of the music. Whereas most piano music assigns the left hand to the lower part of the register and the right to the upper, and piano music is so written that one hand often assists the other, Cage conceived each hand as a separate individual, capable of performing in any part of the instrument's enormous range. Crossing over one other constantly during performance, the two hands compose a duet of interpenetrating musical lines anywhere and everywhere on the piano: an elegant, balletic display that no audio recording of the work can convey. Cage therefore transformed the solitary nature of solo music into a social one.

The sounds of the *Etudes Australes* encompass an extraordinarily wide range – all manner of sounds in every register and chords of all

John Cage, *Etudes Australes* (1974–5), excerpt.

types, from diminished and major or minor triads to others far more dissonant. The variety confounds any attempt to make narrative sense from the music as it unfolds. Instead each sonority is best savoured one after the other, appreciated if they suggest something (or not) and forgotten as soon as the next sound occurs. Although the etudes differ audibly from one other after a few hearings, the differences become strangely unimportant – seeing the stars, one does not measure the distance between them, or quantify their brightness. Occasionally patterns might suggest themselves, but not seeing them does not diminish the individual stars' fundamental beauty. Silence, slightly enhanced by the bass tones that sympathetically vibrate, gives the space necessary to separate each experience from the next, while still binding them together.

If the etudes metaphorically demonstrated the heroism of the individual, another new commission would make a more critical statement through the words of many individuals speaking at the same time. *Lecture on the Weather* (1975), made in response to a request from the Canadian Broadcasting Corporation, was the first of several pieces commissioned from Cage to celebrate the US bicentennial celebrations of 1976. But the occasion gave him the opportunity to make a work more akin to outright protest. The score includes his stated preference that the twelve performers should be Canadians that had once held US citizenship. (Canada was a haven for draft dodgers throughout the Vietnam era.) Cage used texts from Thoreau – *Walden*, the *Essay on Civil Disobedience* and the *Journal* – and made selections of them through chance operations. The sound of the twelve speakers was complemented by recordings of natural sounds created by Maryanne Amacher, and Luis Frangella furnished slides – negatives of Thoreau's drawings – that flashed on and off like lightning during the performance.

To make his dissent explicit, Cage specified that – before any performance – a preface be read that contains many withering remarks about polity in general and the USA in particular:

I began to realize that what is called balance between the branches of our government is not balance at all: all the branches of our government are occupied by lawyers. . . . Our political structures no longer fit the circumstances of our lives. Outside the bankrupt cities we live in Megalopolis which has no geographical limits. Wilderness is global park. I dedicate this work to the USA that it may become just another part of the world, no more, no less.[16]

The works that Cage made for himself to perform during the 1970s represented a much broader perspective on his social beliefs. *Child of Tree* (1975) describes a method by which one uses an amplified cactus to produce a kind of improvised music free from the reliance on the performer's taste and memory. He thought of this and similar works – including *Branches* (1976) and *Inlets* (1977) – as a 'music of contingency' because the organic materials functioning as musical instruments were unpredictable; the cactus, for instance, quickly deteriorated and needed to be replaced with a new one that behaved differently in performance.[17]

Perhaps Cage's greatest solo work was one he had begun to make for himself a year before *Child of Tree*. *Empty Words*, completed in 1975, is a vast text composition intended for concert performance; indeed, he specifically claimed that it represented 'a transition from literature to music'.[18] Drawing from Thoreau's *Journal*, Cage traces a steady process of semantic extirpation throughout the work's four parts. Part 1, for instance, contains no complete sentences:

> bon pitch to a truer wordgenerally the
> shoal and weedy places
> by her perserverancekind velled
> no longer absorbed ten
> succeededbetween the last hoeing
> and the digging a mica many
> of swampsaio against its white body[19]

By the end of part 4, spaces of varying lengths separate single letters or small groups of letters:

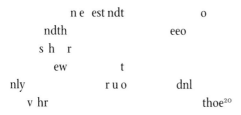

As Cage explained, part 4 allows for three sonic possibilities: a series of letters; a series of letters and silences; and a series of silences.[21] The size of the spaces indicates the approximate length of the silences.

Cage performed excerpts from *Empty Words* throughout the 1970s, and few works of his engendered such feelings of aversion from his audiences. He premiered part 4 on 8 August 1974 – coincidentally, the same day that Richard Nixon formally announced his resignation as President of the United States – at the Naropa Institute (now Naropa University), a centre of learning founded in the same year that combined principles of traditional Western instruction with contemplative education derived from Eastern practices, especially meditative Buddhism. As slides of Thoreau drawings were slowly projected, Cage performed the work at a small table with his back to the audience, who responded by filling the numerous silences with catcalls, guitar playing, screams and whistles.[22]

In a brief question and answer session following the performance, Cage pulled no punches, registering his extreme disgust with the audience's behaviour. After characterizing the catcalls as 'mere stupid criticisms', he added that 'the thing that made a large part of the public's interruption this evening so ugly was that it was full of self-expression'. When asked if he was pleased that the audience had responded to his work honestly, Cage retorted, 'If we are talking about the interruptions, that's not to be classified under honest, that's to be classified under the complete absence of self-control and openness to boredom – and boredom comes not from without but from within.'[23] Something similar happened in December 1977 when Cage performed the work's third part at a notorious concert in Milan. The performance lasted for well over two hours without an interval, and the audience, who began to become restless around ten minutes into the event, expressed its displeasure in successive waves, each more violent than the first. Like the dissenters at the retrospective concert of 1958, they first attempted to bring the concert to an end with over-enthusiastic applause; when this failed to work, they resorted to something resembling a riot worthy of the 1968 student protests.[24]

Considered superficially, Cage's consternation – especially at the Naropa event – implied his continuing allegiance to the former hierarchy obtaining between master-artist and disciple-audience, a non-interactive situation in which the audience remained reverent and silent. But he correctly dismissed the audience's claims that their uproar constituted a creative response intended to complement his own, identifying it instead as a sustained effort to silence his words through brutish force. The difference between the two positions – Cage as transcendent genius demanding unconditional respect and Cage as individual hoping to express himself without the expectation of oppressive resistance – is subtle but crucial. In anarchistic communities individuals consent not to crush the singular expression of any other member of the group. Cage's understanding of anarchism held that audience and performer consent to the social contract that brings them together for the event; the audience's communication of disapproval during the Naropa performance violated that contract.

The large ensemble works from the 1970s represented equally new possibilities for social organization and led to equally negative responses. Following the discovery of *Cheap Imitation* – its simplicity, its lack of pretension – Cage conceived a new kind of orchestral music. He created orchestral arrangements of the piece that obligated orchestral players to play the same line together, and in a circumstance that they would maintain their sense of ensemble not through a conductor but through listening to each other, as chamber musicians do. But unlike chamber music, the music of this piece was a single line, deceptively simple and devoid of any technical device that the musicians could hide behind. By performing such music, Cage hoped that their devotion to simplicity would change their minds.

Naturally the Dutch musicians who in May 1972 planned to give the premiere were totally unprepared for the challenges. Orchestral musicians are accustomed to practise an unfamiliar composition only when its difficulties are obvious. Faced with Cage's transparent music, they must have felt that sight-reading at the rehearsal would be sufficient. The conductor was similarly unprepared. Cage remained adamant that the arrangement – this one for 24 players – be performed as he intended, and so the premiere consisted solely of a rehearsal of the first movement. When the Dutch promised Cage a future performance, something worse happened: 'After hearing a few miserable attempts to play the first phrases, I spoke to the musicians about the deplorable state of society (not only of musical society), and I withdrew the piece from the evening's program.'[25] Thereafter Cage would insist on extensive rehearsal time for performances of the work. Still, the lesson was learned. He would never again make an orchestral piece quite like *Cheap Imitation*.

Two later compositions explore further the implications of Cage's *Musicircus* concept. That work, as described in chapter Four, consisted solely of an open invitation to musicians of many backgrounds, probably many different levels of skill, to congregate at a specific location and play whatever music they wished without paying attention or responding to any of the other music they heard around them. The resulting cacophony, which Cage called a 'circus situation', removed the individual identities and intentions of the performers by multiplying the number of sound sources.

In another commission for the American bicentennial – *Apartment House 1776* (1976) – Cage revisited the musicircus concept. But in this work his compositional choices created a more nuanced kind of musicircus in which identity – with all of its possibilities for rich semantic association – could appear just briefly enough that it registered without losing the sense of multiplicity Cage favoured.

For *Apartment House,* Cage assembled a variety of materials: drum solos from an eighteenth-century collection, a few short tunes of the period, and an array of new music he made called 'harmonies': taking as source material eighteenth-century hymnody from such compos- ers as William Billings, he used chance operations to unmoor the strongly directional quality of the simple harmony in the pieces. The result sounds as if remnants of the hymns are floating in space; they retain their flavour and a semblance of their original expression, but sound utterly fresh.

Against this elaborate backdrop, four singers representing four distinct national traditions – a Native American, an African American, a Sephardic Jew and an Anglo-American – sing the sacred music of their respective peoples. Hence the Apartment House aspect: one dwelling serves as home to many people, many different backgrounds, many different possibilities.[26]

Listening to the piece results in a host of various impressions. The perky eighteenth-century tunes and drum cadences lend a festive atmosphere to the work, while the slow-moving harmonies sound like echoes from the past – amiable and nostalgic. More poignant still is the superimposition of Negro spirituals and Protestant hymnody, Native American song and Sephardic chant: an intermingling of faith and the profound promise of shared humanity. A pessimist can read the piece as a hopeless jumble of musics that does violence to each. Allen Hughes's review of the first New York Philharmonic performance, which reported that hundreds of subscribers made a mad dash for the door as soon as the work began, suggests this interpretation:

> the cacophony of it all was more than the conservative members of the Philharmonic public could take. People who would normally be expected to have good manners apparently gave no thought to others as they pushed their way past seated neighbors to make their ways to the aisles.
>
> Despite the massive exodus, the like of which this reporter has never witnessed in 25 years of professional concert-going, the great majority of the audience stayed to the end of the work, which lasts more than half an hour, and, at the end, cheered or booed enthusiastically.[27]

For an optimist, the music suggests the hopefulness of Cage's anarchism, a chance for very different people with very different beliefs to coexist, to be equally heard and equally valued in synchronic magnificence.

Cage, who was surprised that some audiences of *Apartment House 1776* did not find the work cheerful, also began to express his displeasure when performers took what he considered unconscionable licences with his work. A year earlier, in the summer of 1975, he famously lashed out following a performance of *Song Books* at the University of Buffalo in what has become one of the most legendary and hotly contested anecdotes in Cage's biography. In the words of composer Peter Gena, who described others' recollections of the event,

> During the performance, Julius [Eastman] had extended his interpretation to slowly undressing his boyfriend on stage. Then, he approached his (Julius's) sister and attempted to do the same thing. His sister responded, 'No Julius, no!' Julius

moved on to something else. The next day during a plenary session John pounded his fist on the desk and shouted, 'I'm tired of people who think that they could do whatever they want with my music!' Everyone has witnessed pieces where performers or composers make fools of themselves, etc., under the 'aegis of Cage'. Too many mistakably thought that John cheerfully accepted such abuses.

In all likelihood it will never be possible to learn exactly what happened during the performance, never mind what triggered his fierce reaction. Gena alluded to the possibility that Cage was offended by the open expression of homosexuality; at the time, he wrote, Cage 'became furious over the most oblique references to homosexuality. He felt that his own personal life was "no one's goddamn business."'[28]

Perhaps Cage's anger in 1974 and 1975 also owed more than a little to his ill health during those years. Although he had stopped smoking earlier in the decade, he still suffered from a host of ailments: blood poisoning, arthritis and mysterious pains behind his left eye, which his doctors could not explain. After complaining to Yoko Ono one day, he was advised by her to consult a woman named Shizuko Yamamoto, who gave him shiatsu massage and directed him to adopt the macrobiotic diet:

Basically my diet is brown rice and beans. Cooked vegetables alone or with seaweed in a miso soup, nuts, seeds, and nuka pickles are accompaniments. Oils, sesame, corn, and olive, take the place of butter. Now and then I eat fish or chicken. No dairy products, sugar, fruits, or meat.[29]

The diet had miraculous effects on his health; he followed it for the rest of his life, occasionally bending the rules to include some fresh fruit or a shot of vodka.

Cage's improving health facilitated his openness to new projects. Already his music had begun to develop along several distinct and sometimes contradictory paths, or what he called 'overlapping layers', from the extreme notational precision in the *Freeman Etudes* to such freer works as *Child of Tree* or *Score (40 Drawings by Thoreau) and 23 Parts* (1974), and from chance composition to the works composed solely through his own taste in works like *Song Books*.[30] With such text works as *Mureau* (1970) and *Empty Words*, Cage had increased his efforts in literature and would continue to do so for the rest of his life. In January 1978 he began a sustained activity in visual art at Crown Point Press in Oakland, California (the organization moved to San Francisco in 1986); in all, he would make around 1,000 artworks: drawings, prints and watercolours.

In addition to the painting he had done in his twenties, Cage completed another important artwork in 1969, *Not Wanting to Say Anything about Marcel*, made with the help of Calvin Sumsion. This work consisted of eight separate series of what Cage called plexigrams – each of which comprised eight Plexiglas rectangles upon which were silkscreened words and images chosen from a dictionary through chance operations. The plexigrams were placed in a wooden base, but could be reordered in any permutation, and he also made two lithographs from two of the plexigrams (again selected by chance operations). Cage's interest in the visual appearance of words had 3 of the *Diary*, which employed various colours and typefaces, and in the *62 Mesostics Re Merce Cunningham* (1971), in which each *letter* appeared in a different typeface and in such widely varying sizes that the work is notoriously difficult to read.

Not Wanting retains some connection to Cage's privileging of process over object by the very mobility of the plexigrams in their wooden base; even the isolated words and images seem to resist the possibility of performance. But the physical beauty of the plexigrams marks a decisive step, for Cage at least, back towards the idea of an art object designed for contemplation, perhaps not unlike *Cheap*

Imitation. Is it possible, then, to respond aesthetically to the imagery and composition of his visual work without becoming trapped within the mentality of art for art's sake? In other words, did Cage make useful visual art? The poet and interdisciplinary scholar Joan Retallack, who published a series of conversations with Cage from his final years, maintains that an awareness of the method by which Cage employed chance operations helps to overcome the sense of materiality and even of representation in the work:

> [In the soup cans of Andy Warhol and the flags of Jasper Johns] there is still some kind of mirroring of our world. Or one could say there's a very obvious – on a representational level – point-ing to things in the world. Whereas the pointing to the world in your work is much more conceptual – a pointing toward the relationships between things, rather than the things themselves. Even pointing to something about the nature of relationship – contingency for example.[31]

More generally, the visual composition of Cage's art and irregularities in the imagery generally suggest some contradiction or anomaly comparable to the apparently chaotic variety in such works as *Etudes Australes*.

For the works at Crown Point, Cage used a variety of techniques familiar in printmaking, including engraving, aquatint and drypoint. He began by adapting his composition *Score (40 Drawings by Thoreau) and 23 Parts* into an etching, literally tracing or more freely copying Thoreau's own images from the score to make *Score Without Parts (40 Drawings by Thoreau): 12 Haiku* (1978); chance operations determined which technique he would use and the colours for the images.[32]

The next series of prints, *Seven-Day Diary (Not Knowing)* (1978), involved Cage making a chance-determined series of marks on copper plates with various techniques without seeing what he was

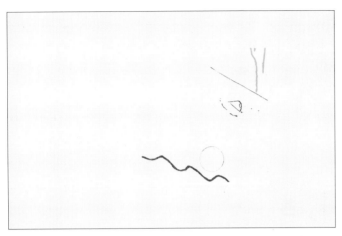

John Cage, *Signals, Artist's Proof 5*, 1978, unique impression, one in a series of 36 related prints (33 x 51 cm on 20 x 30 cm sheet), printed by Lilah Toland at Crown Point Press.

doing; in this manner, he allowed the marks to emerge, insofar as possible, 'as themselves', without his authorial intervention. As work proceeded on the series, he added additional possibilities such as the presence of photographic images, different sizes of the marks made, and colour.[33] Eventually, Cage employed chance operations to determine such variables as the placement and rotation of images, the selection from a larger number of etching techniques, and complex mixtures of colours.

By contrast, when making the series *Signals* (1978), Cage became proficient at one of the most difficult printmaking techniques, the direct engraving of lines into a copper plate by pushing into the metal with a sharp tool. The images of *Signals* include circles, straight lines and photographs of Thoreau drawings; these works appear much more sparse than the *Seven-Day Diary* and demonstrate an elegance and finesse indicating the growing confidence of the artist.

In 1979 Cage and Cunningham moved from Bank Street into a large loft at the corner of West 18th Street and 6th Avenue. The

John Cage working at his loft on 18th Street, New York City.

spacious dwelling permitted Cage to amass a growing number of plants – eventually numbering some 200 – allowing him to bring a sense of the outdoors he cultivated at Stony Point into the thick of Manhattan. He became enchanted by the sound of constant traffic, which he imagined as music while he slept. Cage appreciated the musical quality of traffic because, like the nature he loved, it inhabited a wide frequency range that could not be treated in discrete steps as with conventional musical instruments.[34]

The famous tendency he had already followed towards overlapping fields of activity became even more pronounced as the 1970s came to a close. Back at Crown Point, Cage began an ambitious series of prints called *Changes and Disappearances* (1979–82), which, with its variety of images, colours and visual density, approached the fantastic complexity of the *Freeman Etudes*. Cage worked with 66 copper plates; chance operations determined which and how many plates would appear in each of the 35 prints. Any time a plate was used, chance frequently determined that it should be engraved with new marks: straight lines, elegant curves and photoetchings appear at myriad angles. Thus, the density and visual detail of the etchings resembled the increasing virtuosity of the etudes. Furthermore, the plates and engraved markings on them were inked with a staggering number of different colours; the final print contained 298 colours in all, while another required a total of 45 plates.[35]

Cage was also involved in the realization of an equally grandiose composition he called _____, _____ _____ *Circus on* _____ , whereby he transformed a work of literature into a new multimedia work of art: Cage's idea resulted in *Roaratorio, an Irish Circus on 'Finnegans Wake'* (1979); the colossal musicircus traced a path through James Joyce's final, confounding, comic novel.

To make the piece Cage took Joyce's book and created a series of concentrated poems from its words: the strophes of Cage's poetry contained a vertical string of capital letters in the middle of each line spelling 'James Joyce'; thus, a dense excerpt of Joyce's words – from the beginning of the book to the end – fanned out to the right and left of this string, making a series of evocative shapes. The new form of poetry became known as mesostics.

For the next step Cage wrote to people around the world to collect recordings of every single sound mentioned in the *Wake*, and Irish musicians were employed to record a series of traditional tunes. The whole – including Cage's own recitation of the poem (called a 'Writing through *Finnegans Wake*') was carefully assembled at IRCAM, the high-tech Paris sound studio and new music laboratory established by Pierre Boulez, so that the collected sounds occurred exactly where they would occur when the highly compressed poem reached the point in the *Wake* where the particular sounds were mentioned.

Roaratorio, which was first heard publicly on 20 October 1979 and broadcast on German radio soon thereafter, was also performed on its own as a concert work and in combination with a dance by Merce Cunningham for his company. The densely woven sonic tapestry includes natural sounds as well as more conventional music: Handel, Beethoven (snippets from the 'Eroica' Symphony and the 'Grosse Fuge') along with the Irish tunes and a variety of other musics – highbrow, lowbrow and everywhere in between. Despite Cage's hopes to include sounds from all over the world, he had to rely on sound effect libraries for at least some of the material: a peal of laughter towards the end of the work, for instance, was a staple in American television and film. And some of the recordings have questionable audio quality: the sounds of water, in particular, seem very artificial. Nevertheless, *Roaratorio* is a grand audio collage that fulfils in every way Cage's hopes for abundance. Connoisseurs of the *Wake* may complain about the simplistic way in which the sounds from the book occur in order, rather like a dictionary or travel guide. But the many sounds – in all their variety and intensity – create a kind of music ultimately more appealing than the cacophony of *HPSCHD*, altogether more novel and indeed more relevant to Cage's aesthetics than almost any of his other works.

While the public at large most likely could not keep track of Cage's most recent work and many musicians continued to perform and record the early music for percussion and prepared piano, his reputation had led him to great acclaim and recognition. He was elected as a Fellow in the American Academy of Arts and Letters in 1978, awarded the Karl Sczuka prize for radio art (for *Roaratorio*) in October 1979 and honoured with the American Music Center Letter of Distinction in December of the same year.

Previously, he had told the interviewer Jeff Goldberg (in 1976) that he had once felt protected by a guardian angel until he had created everything he was obligated to produce, but no longer did; ruefully, he added, 'Therefore I could just as well die. Nothing much would be lost if I did.'[36] He was wrong; in the final phase of his career, Cage created new works of a sort he had not made before, and some of these works number among his greatest.

6

Parting

By 1980 the world of contemporary Western classical music hardly resembled the one Cage knew in 1933. The tumult of the 1960s influenced a number of composers to question every assumption about what made new music new: some, like George Crumb and Peter Maxwell Davies, recuperated the sounds and affect of the past through liberal quotations of Bach, Handel and Beethoven; others, such as Steve Reich and Philip Glass, moved away from the rhythmic and harmonic complexities of their predecessors to produce the repetitive and visceral style known as minimalism. Composers of an older generation remained seemingly unaffected by recent developments: Milton Babbitt's extensions of Schoenberg's ideas progressed to scintillating levels of complexity, and Cage himself continued his commitment to the characteristics of music that he, like Babbitt, believed represented modernity: post-tonality and formal innovation. Many younger composers expressed a growing interest in jazz and rock, claiming that these vernacular styles could and should inform any art music that truly speaks to contemporary culture. Indeed, the rapid advances in the technology of mass media since 1950 made this music widely known.

As ever, Cage's observations on the cultural situation of his time demonstrated sensitivity to his environment and a canny prescience. Some twenty years before the first smartphone he wrote, 'shortly everyone, whether he's a musician or not, will have a computer in his pocket'. In 1980, answering a question on whether more composers would come to adopt chance composition, he replied,

> No, I think we're going in a multiplicity of directions. If I performed any function at all, it's one that would have been performed in any case: to take us out of the notion of the mainstream of music, and into a situation that could be likened to a delta or field or ocean, that there are just countless possibilities.[1]

Because his own music had for some time developed along several distinct stylistic paths, Cage represented this delta in microcosm. Increasingly he also devoted much of his energy to making visual art and text composition.

He wrote and performed texts, in part, out of necessity: the debilitating arthritis from which he had suffered for years made it increasingly difficult for him to perform as a pianist. However, the text compositions might also have appealed to him because of the sonic potential of the voice – unconstrained by the discrete steps of a tempered Western musical scale and rich with tone colour, Cage's voice became his ideal instrument.[2]

His late writings departed from the collage technique of the *Diary* and the beleaguered pessimism about world affairs. But even though Cage now expressed renewed optimism, even serenity, he also practised a form of obscurity via an inscrutable textual web made from his own and other people's words. In the third week of January 1980, following a visit to Crown Point Press, he attended a writers' symposium on Ponape in the Caroline Islands organized by Kathan Brown of Crown Point and her husband, Tom Marioni. There, he made a twelve-minute text composition called *Themes & Variations*.[3]

A series of mesostics on the names of various individuals important to him (including David Tudor and Robert Rauschenberg), Cage's poetry related not to his mentors and friends but rather to a number of ideas associated with his work, such as 'Devotion',

'Anarchy' and 'Love = space around loved one'. Once he completed the mesostics, he used chance operations to redistribute the lines of poetry without disturbing the central mesostic string. For instance, the first of the mesostics he wrote using Tudor's name reads:

we Don't know

whAt

we'll haVe

when we fInish

Doing

whaT we're doing

bUt

we know every Detail

Of

pRocess

we're involveD in

A way

to leaVe no traces

nothIng in between

herDed ox

When chance operations intermingled lines from the remaining four mesostics for Tudor's name, only the first, sixth, thirteenth and fourteenth lines from the original mesostic remain (as seen overleaf).

The resulting mix of lines created what Cage called 'renga'. Conventional renga poetry, Cage explained, comprises at least 36 five-line stanzas, each of which follows a syllable count of 5–7–5–7–7; more important, the poetry is written collaboratively:

Successive lines are written by different poets. Each poet tries to make his line as distant in possible meanings from the preceding line as he can take it. This is no doubt an attempt to open the minds of the poets and listeners or readers to other relationships than those ordinarily perceived.[4]

```
                we Don't know
                  At dawn
                 and Valley
                   thIngs
                   to Do

             whaT we're doing
        zen becomes confUsing
         south sea islanD

                  mOuntain

          mountain bReeze

                   Desert

                   lAke

             to leaVe no traces
             nothIng in between
             no neeD⁵
```

In using chance operations to create the admixture of ideas, Cage dispensed with a community of poets but retained what he felt was essential to renga. He viewed this work and others following it as 'a way of writing which comes from ideas, is not about them, but which produces them.'[6]

As Cage approached his 70th birthday in 1982, soloists and ensembles presented his work or, with increasing frequency, commissioned new compositions. He continued to perform with the Merce Cunningham Dance Company both in nationwide and European tours, including a number of near-annual engagements in London at Sadler's Wells Theatre. The constant travel these events involved gave him very little time to compose; nevertheless, he managed to complete two large orchestral works: *Thirty Pieces for Five Orchestras* (1981) and *Dance/4 Orchestras* (1982), the latter commissioned for the Cabrillo Festival of Contemporary Music in Santa Cruz, California.

Two of the many retrospective concerts from 1982 demonstrated incredible enthusiasm for Cage's personality and music. In Wall-to-Wall John Cage and Friends (presented 13 March at New York's Symphony Space from 11 a.m. until 1:15 the next morning), a large audience saw both new and old works. The pianist Margaret Leng Tan, who had begun working extensively with Cage in 1981, opened the marathon concert; her performance of *Bacchanale* (1940) and *In the Name of the Holocaust* (1942) included a strongly choreographic aspect that enlivened these early works. Cage himself participated in a performance of *Speech 1955* (1955), walking through the auditorium with a boombox and an unshakable grin. Britain's Almeida International Festival of Contemporary Music devoted three days to his work in late May: the events included a concert performance of *Roaratorio* (1979), John Tilbury performing the *Sonatas and Interludes for Prepared Piano* (1946–8) and a Cageian musicircus comprising *Atlas Eclipticalis* (1961–2), *Song Books* (1970) and other works.[7]

National and international awards continued to recognize his artistic achievement, including the New York Mayor's Award of Honor for Arts and Culture in 1981 and his appointment as Commandeur de l'Ordre des Arts et des Lettres from the French ministry of culture in 1982. When he performed his own work at such events, he almost invariably chose a text composition, especially excerpts from *Empty Words* (1973–4). Perhaps the events aroused a retrospective mood in him as well. As part of the International Dance Course for Professional Choreographers and Composers in Guildford, Surrey, Cage made *Composition in Retrospect* (1981), a series of mesostics on words related to guiding principles in his music including 'method', 'discipline' and 'indeterminacy'; though primarily a poetic meditation on his compositional practice, it opens with a brief passage on the contingency of his recollections: 'My / mEmory / of whaT / Happened / is nOt / what happeneD'.[8] He performed this work often and it figured prominently as a source for one of his greatest text works, *I–VI* (1988), delivered at Harvard University on the occasion of his appointment as Charles Eliot Norton Professor of Poetry for the 1988–9 academic year.

Around the same time, Cage also began to acknowledge recordings, which he had long opposed, as a medium through which to disseminate noteworthy performances of his recent music. He became friendly with a man named Brian Brandt through their mutual attendance at many concerts during this time; Brandt recalled that he established the American recording label Mode Records in order to make available a performance by Michael Pugliese and Frances-Marie Uitti of Cage's *Etudes Boreales* (1978).[9] Beginning in 1984, Cage supervised the recording himself, which was issued as Mode's first release. He later oversaw other recordings of both old and recent works, perhaps with a view to documenting his musical legacy in a more permanent way; an eleven-performer account of his *Atlas Eclipticalis* became Mode's second release.

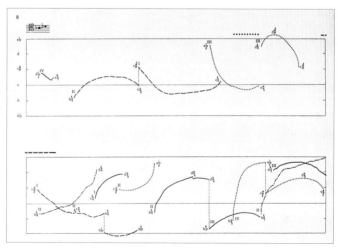

John Cage, *Ryoanji*, excerpt from version for bass.

Cage's musical composition between 1980 and 1985 does not always approach the high quality of his works in visual art and text from the same years. The conceptions for several compositions owe to ideas he had already explored in visual art. *Ryoanji* (1983–5), one of Cage's best works from this period, originated in artwork he made for a French edition of one of his books. The art alludes to the rock garden at the Ryōan-ji temple in Kyoto, which consists of fifteen stones placed in an expanse of raked sand. For the musical works, each page shows flowing curves that Cage produced by tracing around stones; the placement of the stones and their tracings were determined through chance operations. These curving shapes correspond to a series of glissandi that are produced by the instrumental soloist; because many pages show intersecting shapes – thus, multiple glissandi occurring simultaneously – the soloist must prepare recordings of himself performing the others, which are played when he presents the work in concert. Many of the curves inscribe extremely small, microtonal pitch ranges; the recordings offer a further, ghostly quality to the sounds. *Ryoanji* can be played with an optional percussion part consisting of repeated ostinatos varying in length and at a tempo so slow that one cannot readily perceive a sense of regular metre.[10]

For the orchestral work *Thirty Pieces for Five Orchestras*, Cage appropriated the method for the print series of *On the Surface* (1980–82). For the scraps of copper Cage used as the basis for imagery in the prints, he substituted a piece of paper the size of an entire page of score, which he then cut into smaller shapes according to chance operations; he used the smaller shapes to locate the position of musical notes and the instruments playing them. When one of the shapes hung over the edge of the music paper, Cage devised a series of repeating ostinatos – in various tempos – to be played by small groups of instruments.

If the one available recorded performance of this work and the single recording of the somewhat later *Etcetera 2/4 Orchestras* (1986) represent the music accurately, Cage's orchestral pieces from this period fall short of such impressive earlier works as *Atlas Eclipticalis* and *Apartment House 1776* (1976). The gestures – particularly the frequent short accented notes in *Etcetera 2* – sound too familiar, too much like avant-garde music from earlier decades that relied on similarly violent outbursts. The fault may lie with performers and the nature of orchestral performance, as Cage had already experienced with the contemptible readings of *Atlas* by the New York Philharmonic in 1964: the players, more invested in the symphonic literature of the nineteenth century and its aesthetic assumptions, take a trivial approach to Cage's music and, lacking any semblance of responsibility, create a mockery of it. Nevertheless, the sonic density of the two orchestral works seems clumsy and inchoate compared with the complexity of the corresponding visual art.

One notational innovation in *Thirty Pieces* became increasingly significant to Cage for the rest of his life. The music for the work was notated in a series of what he called time brackets, a kind of musical measure giving performers a certain amount of freedom regarding when they could begin and end playing the contents within it. At the left-hand side and above the musical staff were inscribed either a single time indication, say 1'30", or a range of time indications such as 26'15 ⟷ 27'00"; at the right-hand side, either a single time (perhaps 3'00") or a second range (for instance, 26'45" ⟷ 27'30"). In the case of the single time indications above, performers began the content within the bracket at 1'30" and had to complete it by 3'00"; ranges of indications allowed performers the freedom to select start- or stop-times within the given ranges. As they performed, they watched a count-up timer either at their music desk or displayed on a screen that all could see.

Cage had used parcels of times in earlier works, most famously in the *Black Mountain Event* (1952), but they were larger slabs of time containing somewhat freer content. With the development of the time brackets, however, he arrived at an elegant solution to his perennial opposition to a conductor who controlled all aspects of the performance. As time went on, Cage experimented with time brackets of various sizes, and later with radically different musical content.[11]

Cage's work in composition changed substantially beginning in December 1983, when he began using a personal computer to facilitate much of his creative process. He was considerably aided by the composer Andrew Culver, who wrote most of the software that Cage used including a simulation of the I Ching coin toss and a utility that generated streams of time brackets for solo and ensemble works. Culver has hypothesized that the automation provided by the computer made it possible for Cage to devote more time to his visual art.[12] In 1984 he began to make a series of works for up to sixteen instruments and voice that could be performed singly or in any combination and which could be excerpted to fit any time duration up to 30 minutes. *Music for* _____ combined the busy, virtuosic gestures of the *Freeman Etudes* (1977–80; 1989–90),

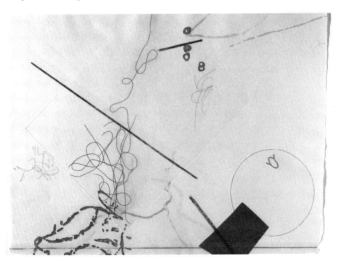

John Cage, *Déreau*, no. 11 (1982), 38 engravings with drypoint, aquatint, and photoetching printed in two impressions each (36 x 48 cm), printed by Lilah Toland at Crown Point Press.

the repeated ostinatos he used in *Thirty Pieces for Five Orchestras* and single tones – all notated within a series of time brackets. Culver's software facilitated his work on these pieces to a great extent.

Cage's activity in visual art during the first few years of the 1980s was dominated by three large sets: *Changes and Disappearances* (1979–82), *On the Surface* and *Déreau* (1982). The latter, whose title is a portmanteau word fashioned from decor and Thoreau, combines photoengraved images from Thoreau's drawings in fixed positions ing positions were determined through chance operations. The colours once again involve complicated mixtures created via chance operations that gradually change over the course of 38 prints.

On his next trip to Crown Point in 1983, Cage brought along a number of stones that he intended to use for a series of prints related to the *Ryoanji* theme. In contrast to the *Ryoanji* music, in which he traced curves from the stones that could be read from left to right in the manner of music, Cage now proposed to place certain stones on copper plates and trace circles around them using the drypoint technique – simply scratching the lines on the copper. Single traces around the stones did not produce a sufficiently striking visual effect, so Cage increased the number of tracings around each stone and was happy with the results. The first works in the series contain approximately fifteen tracings around the stones; later ones increased the number to hundreds and, in the final series, over 3,000. The tracings themselves show a number of irregularities in density and give the impression of a dense, portentous web of images. Cage continued to produce pencil drawings using the same technique until he died.[13]

After a one-year hiatus, Cage returned to Crown Point Press in 1985. During this visit, he began various experiments involving fire and branding. Cage and his assistants built a fire with newspaper in the bed of the printing press and ran damp paper through it; this process extinguished the fire and left the imprints of swirling smoke on the paper. Afterward, he branded the smoked paper with marks from hot teapots. These works led to a very beautiful series from the following year, *Eninka*. In this series Cage used a single link from a large iron chain to brand sheets of gampi, an extremely thin Japanese paper; this paper was so delicate that it would often take on images of words from the newspapers used in the smoking process.[14] The earth tones of the paper and the simplicity of the branded circle give *Eninka* a sense of emptiness that he would soon explore in much of his final music.

In 1988 Cage began the first of two extended studio visits to the Miles C. Horton, Sr. Research Center at Mountain Lake, Virginia, where he produced a number of visual works using watercolours. The visit was organized by Ray Kass, an art professor at Virginia Polytechnic and State University, and grew out of an impromptu studio practice that Kass arranged in 1983 after seeing Cage's *Ryoanji* prints and drawings. Kass, who was impressed by Cage's drawing technique and the unconventional nature of the works, thought that Cage might enjoy working with watercolour. Cage was guardedly optimistic but agreed to participate. As before, Cage focused on stones, now selecting a number of large, smooth stones from the nearby New River. He painted around these with various brushes made from feathers, and the resulting images show lovely curving strokes in which the colour is occasionally streaked with white.[15] Cage made a second visit in 1990 to produce the series *River Rocks and Smoke*; here, paintings around the stones adorn smoked paper and so harmonize with the sparseness of the prints from the later 1980s.

The final works at Crown Point Press demonstrated a general tendency towards ever increasing restraint. In *Smoke Weather Stone Weather* (1991), the delicate tracings of stones (now made with a variety of techniques including sugar lift and spit bite aquatint) seem almost of a piece with the richly textured contours of the smoked paper. *Without Horizon* (1992) simplifies the process even further: the grey paper shows, not circles, but rather simpler marks along one edge of

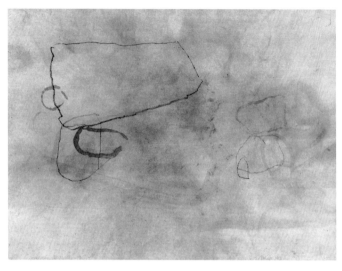

John Cage, *Smoke Weather Stone Weather* 19 (1991), one in a series of 37 unique aquatints with etching on smoked paper (40 x 51 cm), printed by Paul Mullowney at Crown Point press.

selected stones, which are printed in fifteen possible varieties of black ink; a sense of gesture is attenuated almost to non-existence.[16]

In addition to the visual artworks, Cage also designed an installation, *Writings Through the Essay: On the Duty of Civil Disobedience* (1985–91) for the Fundació Espai Poblenou in Barcelona; since 1998 this has been installed on the topmost floor of Kunsthalle Bremen, Germany. Thirty-six sound sources transmit Cage's computer-processed reading of the *Voiceless Essay* (1985), his writing through of Thoreau's essay; the installation includes 24 lights and six chairs that are positioned in the space through chance operations. He also helped to organize such exhibits as the Museum Circle, in which various Munich museums contributed works for a show in the Bayerische Staatsgemäldesammlungen, the placement of which were determined by chance operations.[17]

Academia began a more intense exploration of Cage in the 1980s, with articles, books and conferences focusing on him. Some of these events included presentations of Cage's music, for instance the Semana John Cage at the Universidad de Puerto Rico from 1–5 March 1982, in which Francis Schwartz, Richard Kostelanetz and Daniel Charles participated. Wesleyan University celebrated his 75th birthday with a more substantial symposium, John Cage at Wesleyan, which took place from 22–27 February 1988; the conference initiated a spate of publications concerning his work. Other conferences followed, including those at the University of New Mexico (27–30 March 1988) and Stanford University (27–31 January 1992).

One of the strongest scholars at the Wesleyan conference was James Pritchett, whose musicological training enabled him to deduce Cage's method from sketch materials, and indeed to discern that Cage's own taste continued to have a role, not only in the designing of the precompositional plans to be acted upon by chance operations, but sometimes also in the actual realization of those plans.[18] In a time when many, if not all, critics and scholars studying Cage celebrated his artistic inscrutability and seemingly limitless interests, Pritchett's argument that he should be understood as a composer first and foremost – extended in a later monograph discussing all his music – proved extraordinarily influential; his example stimulated other scholars to focus more attention on Cage's working methods, resulting in studies of text and visual works along with music.[19]

Cage's final works acted both as a response and as a counterpoint to his growing accolades. For Wesleyan he made *Anarchy* (1987), another of his mesostic compositions. He drew upon a variety of sources by anarchistic writers (including Peter Kropotkin, Thoreau and Emma Goldman) as well as such miscellany as an amusing graffito noticed by Culver, 'US OUT OF CENTRAL AMERICA + PUERTO RICO + MANHATTAN'. Culver's computerized I Ching software generated hexagram numbers that Cage used to select which source text or texts would be used as well as which central mesostic string appeared (these included names of authors and titles of books in addition to the texts themselves). Then, with the aid of another software utility, MESOLIST (written by Jim Rosenberg), the computer generated twenty mesostics. The resulting poetry leaves behind tantalizing echoes of the original texts:

> New living
> necessary buT
> what Each individual does his actions
> exist aMong the
> new social relationshiPs it is the
> revoLution is the constitution of
> of people ceAses
> socieTy's
> nEw
> iS more and more passing away [20]

As ever, the poetry suggested neither a course of action nor a conventionally poetic evocation of anarchistic ideas, but something in between: an actual example, perhaps, of what life and thought might become within an anarchistic community of individuals.

Much of Cage's music after 1985 equalled the stature of the late text pieces. Responding to a commission from a German couple who had long championed his work, Heinz-Klaus Metzger and Rainer Riehn, Cage made *Europeras 1 & 2* (premiered 1987); in this work singers perform excerpts of their choice from the eighteenth- and nineteenth-century operatic repertory within a series of time brackets. Frequently many singers perform at the same time; the orchestra adds an accompaniment that Cage prepared by subjecting various orchestral parts from well-known operas to chance operations.

Metzger and Riehn hoped that the work would utterly demolish the tradition of opera; Cage, always thinking positively, ended up creating a celebration of the medium that frequently indulged in a sense of nostalgia almost in spite of itself. Following the premiere of the work – which was delayed when an arsonist burned down the opera house and which was marked by the orchestra musicians' wilful disregard for their carefully prepared parts – he made two further works for smaller forces (singers, pianists and musicians performing pre-recorded opera discs with vintage phonographs), *Europeras 3 & 4* (1990) and *Europera 5* (1991).

New works for the Merce Cunningham Dance Company, as always, stimulated Cage's best efforts. In *Sculptures Musicales* (1989), he envisioned a series of sonic sculptures sounding, one after another, from various locations in the theatre; in performance, these sculptures tended to be created through electronic means, and their deafening volume and unpredictable occurrence frightened and annoyed the dancers as they performed Cunningham's *Inventions* alongside it.

Meanwhile, using the time-bracket technique, Cage now explored extreme transparency of material and, quite often, extremely long durations. Although he had initially expected that his *Music for* _____ series would proceed indefinitely, he stopped creating new parts after hearing a performance of all seventeen in 1987. Around the same time, he began making a series of over 40 works whose title referred only to the number of performers involved. The first, *Two* (1987), was scored for flute and piano. As Cage wrote additional works for the same number of performers, he added a superscript Arabic numeral to distinguish one from the others; for instance, *Two^6* (1992), spoken as 'Two Six', was a duet for violin and piano. For Cunningham's *Beach Birds*, a lyrical ensemble piece in which the dancers' slow motion and placid stillness are suddenly interrupted by bursts of running, jumping and elegant spinning, he made *Four^3* (1991), which contains the evocative rustlings of rainsticks, a long-sustained high pitch (on violin or an electronic oscillator), and extremely slow, unaccompanied melodies played on two pianos positioned at some distance from each other.

As before, Cage made several of these so-called Number Pieces with his own performance obligations in mind, taking into account his physical limitations. His health had become even more precarious since 1985, when he suffered a minor stroke; he also was plagued by an extremely acute case of eczema, which substantially abated a year before he died through an experimental treatment. *One³* (1989), subtitled *4'33" No. 2*, called for a performer to raise the level of amplification in a space to the maximum level before distortion occurs; he then joined the audience to listen to the electronically enhanced ambience for an indeterminate length of time. Cage performed this work in November 1989 in conjunction with his receiving the Kyoto Prize, an international award endowed by the Japanese Inamori Foundation recognizing significant contributions to the scientific, cultural and spiritual betterment of mankind.[21]

In many of the Number Pieces, Cage directly confronted his long-standing opposition to his old nemesis, harmony; he had been influenced in this regard by works of contemporaries exploiting sonic relationships in great detail, including James Tenney's *Critical Band* – in which a single tone played by a number of instruments gradually widens microtonally to include a band of frequencies – and Pauline Oliveros's examples of what she called 'deep listening', which 'cultivates appreciation of sounds on a heightened level, expanding the potential for connection and interaction with one's environment, technology and performance with others in music and related arts'.[22] As a result of these experiences, Cage developed the idea of what he called anarchic harmony, a harmony that obeys no rules but, instead, consists simply in noticing sounds as they happen to occur together.[23]

One of the greatest Number Pieces, *Two²* (1989), was written for the pianists Edmund Niemann and Nurit Tilles performing together as the piano duo Double Edge. In it, Cage brilliantly united anarchic harmony with the principles of renga poetry. He expressed the renga idea in *Two²* in several ways: first, each line of music is divided into five measures to correspond with the five lines of the poetry. The first measure contains five separate musical events – chords or single tones, usually shared between the two pianists – analogous to the five syllables of the first line; the second measure has seven events and so on. And there are a total of 36 such five-measure sections in the piece. The pianists proceed one measure at a time. They must read the music in their respective measures from left to right; and while they can take any amount of time to perform a measure, each pianist must wait until both have finished the same measure before proceeding to the next. In this manner, the ordering of the 'syllables' composing one 'line' almost always occurs in a somewhat predictable order.[24]

One finds all manner of sonorities in this work: dissonant chords cohabitate amicably with simple triads and ambiguous, neutral single tones. Some sonorities are sublime, while others suggest the result of harsh, even unformed compositional technique. Every time a listener settles into the mode of Cage's discourse, some unexpected sound – a simple seventh chord or even a seemingly banal augmented triad – suddenly intrudes, throwing her off balance and disorienting her reactions. And yet that mingling of so-called incompatible elements is fundamental to Cage's aesthetic and the very source of its magic. This mixture of the generic and the exquisite evokes what Cage admired in Marcel Duchamp's work, its ability to resist becoming a mere 'art object', though Cage was rarely able to achieve a Duchampian ideal.[25]

More interesting, however, is the fact that so many chords – even identical successions of chords – recur in the piece. Their overall unfolding, of course, is determined by chance procedures and performance, which guarantee a nebulous ordering that defies complete predictability.[26] The logic of recurrence in *Two²* resembles not so much conventional musical development as the manner in which friends and acquaintances pass in and out of people's lives – continuity, in other words, that may not make conventional sense but remains meaningful nevertheless.

Much of Cage's thoughts and final day-to-day activities were beautifully documented in a series of interviews with Joan Retallack. She lovingly transcribed every instance of the telephone ringing, every time that Cage used the word 'hmm' when punctuating his sentences (and he used the word often), every time they laughed, even the sounds of Andrew Culver doing work for him and the occasional visits from friends, colleagues and his beloved cat, Losa.[27] More poignantly, she also documented a terrifying experience on 11 July 1992, when Cage was mugged in his own home by a drug addict posing as a UPS delivery person; the experience shook him momentarily, but he decided to continue much as he had before – now aided by friends who thereafter safeguarded him from possible harm.[28]

During his final year of 1992, Cage was extraordinarily busy. In addition to his work at Crown Point in January, he participated in a symposium, John Cage at Stanford: Here Comes Everybody, at Stanford University. In addition to a series of presentations by a number of scholars in literature, philosophy and other fields, Cage reunited for the last time with an old friend, Norman O. Brown, who had shaped Cage's thinking on a number of topics. The two had become estranged in recent years due, in part, to a 1988 paper Brown delivered at Wesleyan in which he accused Cage of being too willing to embrace a contemplative, Apollonian sensibility in his art.[29] At the Stanford symposium, Brown called particular attention to Cage's optimism that persisted in contrast to the imminent possibility of Cage's own death. Retallack remembers an extraordinary exchange between the two men:

John Cage and Losa, 1991.

'I do not believe that the past and the present are all here; and that is related to my perception of death . . . Death is everywhere present in this room', [Brown] said, turning to look directly at Cage. Cage smiled sweetly, saying, 'Nobby, I'm ready.'[30]

His last performance took place on 23 July when he performed one of the parts of his *Four*[6] (1992) along with the composer Joan La Barbara (for whom he had made the vocal part of *Music for* _____), Leonard Stein (a pianist who had studied with Schoenberg and had served as the director of UCLA's Arnold Schoenberg Institute) and a percussionist teaching at Mills College, William Winant. Cage described his own contribution to the work as 'shocking sounds' – the inimitable vocal music that he had first discovered in *Empty Words*. He suffered a massive cerebral haemorrhage on 11 August and died the following day at St Vincent's Hospital. Work begun before he died remained unfinished; birthday celebrations became memorial services.

It is tempting to speculate that Cage, ready for death, anticipated the event through the extreme emptiness of his final works such as *Without Horizon* and the orchestral *Seventy-four* (1992), in which one half of the orchestra slowly plays through a series of a few pitches while the other half plays through a different one. In actuality, he continued to contradict himself even in his final compositions. His last completed work, *Thirteen* (1992), consisted of time brackets containing long, restless melodies, and he also hoped to make a concerto for a silent television soloist accompanied by twelve radios.[31]

These contradictions indicate the lengths Cage would take towards perpetuating the avant-garde in an age when truly shocking art had become increasingly difficult to imagine. David Revill, in his pioneering biography, lamented that the avant-garde had ceased to exist by the time of Cage's death, and that the years since the 1980s had proved more recuperative than revolutionary.[32] But the avant-garde, and supremely the one that John Cage imagined, consists not in a method or a style but, rather, a habit of mind. Revolution continues so long as the artist maintains a curious spirit and the willingness to make unfortunate mistakes alongside sublime discoveries. The avant-garde, as Cage demonstrated over and over again, must always mean something other than what it once was.

Epilogue

Although a panoramic assessment of Cage's life and career in all its complexity – including its successes and failures – is beyond the scope of this book, a few critical remarks may serve to support the claim that, in spite of the complexities and paradoxes of Cage's artistic project, the immensity of his continuing influence rivals that of the most significant artists in the twentieth century.

Cage's complexity resides not least in his own heterogeneity – his famous, cheerful restlessness – which, in turn, accounts for the great number of extraordinary misunderstandings his work has provoked and for the tendency to view askance or to minimize one or another of his creative activities. For years – well into the 1980s – Cage's chance and indeterminate music was largely ignored, his work during those years regarded principally as philosophy of music. The critic John Rockwell's observations are typical: 'But not all of [Cage's music], especially the music of the past twenty-five years, has been very interesting to *hear*: neither "ear music" nor "eye music" but, perhaps, "head music", in that it seemed most interesting as ideas for pieces rather than as pieces *per se*.'[1] Without a clear explanation of the intricate way Cage employed chance operations, performers, audiences, composers and critics obsessed neurotically on the works that brought him fame – *4'33"* (1952), the *Concert for Piano and Orchestra* (1958), *HPSCHD* (1969) – or, worse, simply discounted everything he wrote after 1949.

Nevertheless Cage had never lacked for supporters, and many of these helped to make a powerful case for his value as a composer. The continuing attention of both professional and casual artists who have formed their own positive opinion of Cage, especially those that pursue creative work in music, writing or art, forms a most important element in Cage's multifaceted reception. These individuals have a greater impact – both positive and negative – on the cultural landscape than perhaps any other comparable group who admires and emulates a more conventional artist. Cage's openness to experimentation gives the best of these artists the licence to think in unusual new ways, to adapt existing materials and techniques to new purposes, or even to invent these anew. One is tempted to say these artists are the ones who continue to remain most faithful to John Cage.

On the other hand, Cage's opaque descriptions of his work, his frequent tendency not to offer clear instructions about the role of performers in his music and his generally light-hearted attitude to art mistakenly give the impression that one can do whatever he wishes, and that the more outlandish and absurd the conclusion, the better.

Among various examples of absurdities rationalized by the mantra, 'Cage would have approved', the German city of Halberstadt's ongoing performance of *Organ²/ASLSP* counts as the one of the most exasperating. Cage made an organ arrangement of his earlier piano piece *ASLSP* (an abbreviation which refers to 'as slowly as possible' as well as to a passage in Joyce's *Finnegans Wake*) for the German organist Gerd Zacher. Later, a group of individuals wondered out loud about the implications of the title, especially since the organ could theoretically sustain tone indefinitely. The Halberstadt project represents the answer to their inquiry.

An organ with a small number of pipes was built in the Burchardi-kirche, which was used as a hog barn in the years following the Second World War, along with an electronic mechanism that would keep air blowing continuously through the pipes when activated.

When the realization commenced in September 2001, the only sound was that of the air; the first pitches could be heard on 5 February 2003, when keys that would normally be activated by human fingers were instead fixed into place by weighted objects, and the first change of tones occurred on 5 July 2004. The organizers also decided that the performance should conclude in 2639, a date equidistant from the year 2000 and 1361, the year in which a previous organ, now long gone, was first installed. The performance relies on donations – not all the pipes that will eventually be needed have been built and installed – and the Halberstadt website cheerfully solicits donations of €1,000, which entitles the donors to a plaque with their names on it on display at the church. Deutsche Welle erroneously reported that Cage himself planned the extraordinary duration of the work; in an interview with the news agency, one of the organizers proudly said, 'It doesn't mean anything; it's just there.'[2]

Sadly, however, the Halberstadt project means quite a bit, and the cultural work it performs has the most alarming consequences with respect to Cage's own practice. For one thing, he almost always viewed his music as intended for performance in real time by human beings. When in 1981 Paul Zukofsky told him that the latest of his *Freeman Etudes* was unplayable, Cage abandoned work on them until the English violinist Irvine Arditti played the existing etudes with such virtuosity that he was inspired to finish the series.[3] And while it is possible to imagine that a group of performers could be assembled to perform *Organ²* for 639 years, it is more difficult to imagine Cage sanctioning anyone to spend that much time on a work from his past: he was always thinking of the present and the future, and it seemed clear that he thought excessive attention devoted to the past solved no real social problems. Furthermore he aspired for his music to have a genuine use in society, and while the attention of the Halberstadt project has reinvigorated the town, long ravaged by economic woes and extremist factionalism, he distanced himself from endorsing any particular, overly specific project, even if it served a noble or morally upright cause. He wanted the social problems of our time to be solved globally and through invention of new things; on balance the Halberstadt project perverts Cage's notion of process into the worst kind of object: an effete monument that no human beings could fully experience within their own lifetimes.

At the same time, however, Cage enthusiasts can sympathize with an element in his work that is frankly and thoroughly subversive. All the scholarly attention that has recently been devoted to his work has the unfortunate tendency to normalize him: to take all the caprice, surprise and shock away and reduce him to a series of carefully worked-out propositions that explain everything neatly away. Cage cannot be, and will never be, explained completely: he will always retain the capacity to infuriate and confound, and even his most poetic achievements will perhaps amuse many more than they inspire.

By contrast, some scholars who have understood Cage's use of chance operations have made somewhat premature explanations of Cage's work and its historical position. Richard Taruskin, for instance, believes that Cage's chance music is best understood solely as a manifestation of the 'zero-hour' mentality that prevailed at the end of the Second World War – in other words, as an expression of the imperative that many avant-garde composers felt to overhaul the language of art through appeals to elaborate pre-compositional plans, scientific or mathematical models or the burgeoning research culture centring around university life.[4]

In Taruskin's view Cage's chance music of the 1950s and after represents the extreme example of absolute music: a musical object stripped of any social utility and intended, in Kant's well-known formulation, for disinterested contemplation. Such music functioned as the object of quasi-religious veneration in nineteenth-century German concert life, where an attitude of strict attentive silence had prevailed since mid-century.

Cage's chance and indeterminate music, Taruskin continued, shackled performers to Cage's aesthetic will, which alternately demanded they perform feats of superhuman virtuosity or restricted their interpretive personal engagement without seeming justification. In short, Taruskin's version of the composer is one of a pitiless megalomaniac who wants to subordinate listeners to his own view of sounds for themselves:

> Sounds that were noise on one side of an arbitrary framing gesture are suddenly music, a 'work of art', on the other side. The esthetic comes into being by sheer fiat, at the drop of a piano lid. The audience is invited – no, commanded – to listen to ambient or natural sounds with the same attitude of reverent contemplation they would assume if they were listening to Beethoven's Ninth.[5]

Much of Taruskin's argument largely depends on a view of Cage that accords best with the overdetermined *Music of Changes* (1951). But by 1958 Cage had distanced himself from that work, having likened it to a Frankenstein monster.[6] Taruskin's neglect of Cage's later chance music weakens his claim considerably.

Nor is it accurate to argue, as Taruskin does, that performers cannot discover new things in the music. As his chief witness, Taruskin quotes Margaret Leng Tan, whom he characterizes as being 'cut out of the fun', her freedom diminished by Cage's chance operations: 'By the time you've worked out all this material, can you really give a spontaneous performance? It's a discovery for him [that is, Cage] if he's hearing it for the first time, but it's not a discovery for me.'[7] This remark has never seemed reconcilable with Tan's passionate commitment to Cage's work; in response, she writes that:

> I made this remark to David Revill in the late 1980s. Little did I know that it would come back to bite me time and time again.

I had unwittingly bestowed a gift on the anti-Cage camp, a barb to add to their arsenal of criticisms leveled against Cage's philosophy and approach to making music.

Two decades have passed. With the hindsight of experience, it weighs increasingly upon me to rectify this statement made impulsively at a time when I was grappling with what indeterminacy entailed.

Cage has said of his later works that they came as a complete surprise to him when he heard them in performance as he did not hear the music in his head when he was composing with chance operations. The performer, on the other hand, has to familiarize him- or herself with the material to mount a responsible performance. It was at this juncture that I made that remark. At the time I was struggling with the challenges posed by the indeterminate work, *One²* for multiple pianos [(1989)], that Cage had made for me.

After a couple of unsatisfactory performances, I realized that it was not enough to simply read the score. It was also necessary to practice and acquaint myself so thoroughly with the material that it became reflex. Achieving this level of familiarity was not an end in itself. Rather, it set me free to draw *spontaneously* and confidently on the reservoir of possibilities *at the moment of performance.* The result would then be a truly indeterminate rendition. And each subsequent non-willful, non-repeatable performance experience would retain an element of surprise for me as performer, co-creator and listener simultaneously. I understood, at last, what Cage meant when he said to me, '. . . play whatever comes to hand when you get to each piano without knowing what you are going to do until you get there.'[8]

The best performers of Cage's music, paradoxically, prepare themselves so well that they remain open to the unexpected – either from themselves or from their environment.

Margaret Leng Tan with John Cage at the Whitney Museum, 1991.

Despite the singularity and brilliance of his ideas, Cage's work and aesthetic after 1950 had limitations. He discouraged all extreme expressions of emotion and physical display; his conception of theatre erased the possibility of actors inhabiting their characters, causing them to become – instead – disembodied, asexual puppets; he never felt a performer's intuition could add anything meaningful to music; and he remained dubious that taste alone could serve as a source for new music. To this extent, Cage's work has not supported the development of a truly new and humanistic art.

However, Cage never wanted to eliminate expression from his work; rather he simply wished not to impose his own particular thoughts and feelings, allowing his performers and audiences to enjoy their own experiences without holding on to them compulsively. The principles of Zen embodied in the experience of his art – love with space around loved one, the ability to feel emotion and release it – remain relevant, even critical today. By fostering these principles, humanity may well develop a new kind of subjectivity leading to the social ideals he hoped for.

References

Introduction

1   See 'Composer Pays for Piece of Silence', CNN [online] , http://articles. cnn.com/2002-09-23/entertainment/uk.silence_1_peters-edition-nicholas-riddle-john-cage-trust?_s=PM:SHOWBIZ (accessed 26 May 2011).

2   For two recent examples, see Kyle Gann, *No Such Thing as Silence: John Cage's '4'33"'* (New Haven, CT, 2010) and James Pritchett, 'What Silence Taught John Cage: The Story of *4'33"*', in *The Anarchy of Silence: John Cage and Experimental Art* (Barcelona, 2009), pp. 166–77.

3   Quoted in John Cage, *Silence: Lectures and Writings* (Middletown, CT, 1961), p. 158.

4   James Pritchett's *The Music of John Cage* (Cambridge, 1993) remains an indispensible source. For a recent survey of recordings, see Rob Haskins, 'John Cage and Recorded Sound: A Discographical Essay', *Notes: The Journal of the Music Library Association*, LXVII/2 (2010), pp. 382–409; see also the selected discography in this volume.

5   John Cage, *I–VI: MethodStructureIntentionDisciplineNotationIndeterminacy-InterpenetrationImitationDevotionCircumstancesVariableStructureNonunder-standingContingencyInconsistencyPerformance* (Cambridge, MA, 1990), p. 258.

6   Richard Taruskin, *The Danger of Music and Other Anti-Utopian Essays* (Berkeley, CA, 2009), pp. 261–79; Joan Retallack, *The Poethical Wager* (Berkeley, CA, 2003); David Carter, 'Surface Noise: A Cageian Approach to Electronica', *Popular Music Online*, 1 (2009), at www. popular-musicology-online.com/issues/01/carter-01.html (accessed 22 March 2011).

7   Leta E. Miller, 'Cultural Intersections: John Cage in Seattle, 1938–1940', in *John Cage: Music, Philosophy, and Intention, 1933–1950*, ed. David W.

Patterson (New York, 2002), pp. 47–82; David W. Patterson, 'Appraising the Catchwords, *c.* 1942–1959: John Cage's Asian-Derived Rhetoric and the Historical Reference of Black Mountain College', PhD dissertation, Columbia University, 1996; James Pritchett, 'Understanding John Cage's Chance Music: An Analytical Approach', in *John Cage at Seventy-Five*, ed. Richard Fleming and William Duckworth (Lewisburg, PA, 1989), pp. 249–61.

1 Becoming

1 See Stephen Schwartz, *From West to East: California and the Making of the American Mind* (New York, 1998), pp. 139–204.

2 In general, dates for events in Cage's life and career follow the exhaustive chronology in Paul van Emmerik, Herbert Henck and András Wilheim, *A John Cage Compendium*, at www.xs4all.nl/~cagecomp/ (accessed 24 June 2005).

3 Thomas J. Hines, '"Then Not Yet 'Cage'": The Los Angeles Years, 1912–1938', in *John Cage: Composed in America*, ed. Marjorie Perloff and Charles Junkerman (Chicago, IL, 1994), p. 71.

4 Richard Kostelanetz, ed., *Conversing with Cage*, 2nd edn (New York, 2002), p. 1; Michael Broyles, 'Art Music from 1860 to 1920', in *The Cambridge History of American Music*, ed. David Nicholls (Cambridge, 1998), pp. 227–32.

5 John Cage, *A Year from Monday: New Lectures and Writings* (Middletown, CT, 1967), p. 20.

6 Hines, '"Then Not Yet 'Cage'"', p. 74.

7 John Cage, *Silence: Lectures and Writings* (Middletown, CT, 1961), p. 88.

8 Kostelanetz, ed., *Conversing with Cage*, p. 2.

9 Ibid., pp. 2–4.

10 Cage, *Silence*, p. 271.

11 John Cage, 'Other People Think', in *John Cage: An Anthology*, ed. Richard Kostelanetz (New York, 1991), p. 46.

12 Ibid., p. 48.

13 Kostelanetz, ed., *Conversing with Cage*, p. 3.

14 John Cage, *Musicage: Cage Muses on Words, Art, Music; John Cage in Conversation with Joan Retallack* (Hanover, NH, 1996), pp. 83–4.

15 Kenneth Silverman, *Begin Again: A Biography of John Cage* (New York, 2010), pp. 8–9.

16 Emmerik et al., chronology at *A John Cage Compendium* (accessed 10 March 2011).

17 Christopher Shultis, 'Cage and Europe', in *The Cambridge Companion to John Cage*, ed. David Nicholls (Cambridge, 2002), pp. 22–3.

18 Walter Gropius et al., *The Theater of the Bauhaus*, trans. Arthur S. Wensinger (Middletown, CT, 1961), p. 85.

19 Quoted in David Revill, *The Roaring Silence: John Cage, A Life* (New York, 1992), p. 37.

20 Cage, *Musicage*, p. 85.

21 Shultis, 'Cage and Europe', p. 23.

22 Cage, *Silence*, p. 273.

23 David W. Bernstein, 'Music I: To the Late 1940s', in *The Cambridge Companion to John Cage*, ed. Nicholls, pp. 63–4.

24 David Nicholls, 'Cowell, Henry', in *Grove Music Online. Oxford Music Online*, at www.oxfordmusiconline.com/subscriber/article/grove/music/06743 (accessed 16 March 2011). See also Henry Cowell, *New Musical Resources*, ed. David Nicholls (Cambridge, 1995).

25 Leta E. Miller, 'Henry Cowell and John Cage: Intersections and Influences, 1933–1945', *Journal of the American Musicological Society*, LIX/1 (2006), p. 51. Cage's own accounts of the premiere usually omit the embarrassing manner in which he performed; see, for instance, 'A Composer's Confessions', in *John Cage, Writer: Previously Uncollected Pieces*, ed. Richard Kostelanetz (New York, 1993), p. 30.

26 Hines, '"Then Not Yet 'Cage'"', p. 86.

2 Audacity

1 Thomas J. Hines, '"Then Not Yet 'Cage'": The Los Angeles Years, 1912–1938', in *John Cage: Composed in America*, ed. Marjorie Perloff and Charles Junkerman (Chicago, IL, 1994), pp. 81 and 84.

2 Leta E. Miller explores the complex web of interaction between the two men in 'Henry Cowell and John Cage: Intersections and Influences, 1933–1941', *Journal of the American Musicological Society*, LIX/1 (2006), pp. 47–112.

3 For more, see Michael Hicks, *Henry Cowell, Bohemian* (Urbana, IL, 2002), pp. 134–43.

4 Henry Cowell, 'Who is the Greatest Living Composer?', *Northwest Musical Herald*, 7 (March–April 1933), p. 7.

5 Joseph N. Straus, *Twelve-Tone Music in America* (Cambridge, 2009), pp. 3–20. Straus describes works by Cage's teacher Adolph Weiss and Wallingford Riegger (discussed below), with whom Cage became acquainted when he lived in New York.

6 Henry Cowell, ed., *American Composers on American Music* (Stanford, CA, 1933), cited in John Cage, 'Counterpoint (1934)', in *Writings about John Cage*, ed. Richard Kostelanetz (Ann Arbor, MI, 2004), p. 15.

7 Cage, 'Counterpoint', pp. 16–17.

8 Maureen Mary, 'Letters: The Brief Love of John Cage for Pauline Schindler, 1934–1935', *ex tempore*, VIII/1 (1996), p. 2.

9 Michael Hicks, 'Cage's Studies with Schoenberg', *American Music*, VIII/2 (1990), p. 126.

10 Kenneth Silverman, *Begin Again: A Biography of John Cage* (New York, 2010), p. 13.

11 Mary, 'Letters', p. 4.

12 Ibid., p. 10. Schindler wrote her letters with a typewriter and generally used lowercase.

13 Ibid., p. 11.

14 The account follows the one given in Hicks, 'Cage's Studies with Schoenberg', pp. 127–30.

15 Ibid., p. 127; Mary, 'Letters', pp. 21–2.

16 From a letter to Weiss quoted in Hicks, 'Cage's Studies with Schoenberg', p. 127.

17 Richard Kostelanetz, ed., *Conversing with Cage*, 2nd edn (New York, 2002), p. 5.

18 The actual source for the remark appears to come from a 1953 letter from Yates to Cage, and the meeting referred to probably occurred a few years before Schoenberg's death. See the evidence presented in Hicks, 'Cage's Studies with Schoenberg', pp. 132–5. Brent Reidy explores why Schoenberg myths became pervasive and continue to be important in 'Our Memory of What Happened is Not What Happened: Cage, Metaphor, and Myth', *American Music*, XXVII/2 (2010), pp. 211–27.

19 John Cage, *A Year From Monday: New Lectures and Writings* (Middletown, CT, 1967), p. 46; John Cage, *Silence: Lectures and Writings* (Middletown, CT, 1961), p. 93.

20 Cage, *Silence*, p. 261.

21 Kostelanetz, ed., *Conversing with Cage*, p. 8.

22 John Cage, 'An Autobiographical Statement', in *John Cage, Writer: Previously Uncollected Pieces*, ed. Richard Kostelanetz (New York, 1993), p. 239.

23 Leta E. Miller, 'Cultural Intersections: John Cage in Seattle, 1938–1940', in *John Cage: Music, Philosophy, and Intention, 1933–1950*, ed. David W. Patterson (New York, 2002), p. 50. My chronology and details of Cage's Seattle years are indebted to the painstaking research reported in Miller's essay.

24 Miller, 'Cultural Intersections', pp. 54–64. (Cage claimed the essay was written in 1937 when it was published in *Silence*, p. 3.) The revised date demonstrates that Cage did not formulate all of his most progressive ideas *ex nihilo*, but rather through more nuanced interactions with intellectual currents around him.

25 John Cage, *Silence*, p. 4. For the Varèse anecdote, see Olivia Mattis, 'Conversation with John Cage, New York City (in Cage's Apartment), 28 July 1988, 4–5:15 p.m.' (unpublished), p. 7. I thank Olivia Mattis for sharing this manuscript with me.

26 John Cage, *Musicage: Cage Muses on Words, Art, Music; John Cage in Conversation with Joan Retallack* (Hanover, NH, 1996), p. 101, pp. 126–7.

27 Cage, *Silence*, pp. 271–2; Cage, *A Year from Monday*, p. 138.

28 For more details on Cage's employment of what he called structural rhythm, see James Pritchett, *The Music of John Cage* (Cambridge, 1993), pp. 13–19.

29 See Tamara Levitz, 'Syvilla Fort's African Modernism and John Cage's Gestic Music: The Story of Bacchanale', *South Atlantic Quarterly*, CIV/1 (2005), pp. 123–49.

30 Cage, *Silence*, p. 12.

31 Virgil Thomson, 'Expressive Percussion', in *John Cage: An Anthology*, ed. Richard Kostelanetz (New York, 1991), p. 72. The review was published 22 January 1945.

32 Kostelanetz, ed., *Conversing with Cage*, p. 12.

33 Hines, '"Then Not Yet 'Cage'"', p. 99.

3 Non-attachment

1 Calvin Tomkins, *The Bride and the Bachelors: The Heretical Courtship in Modern Art* (New York, 1965), p. 96.

2 See David W. Patterson, 'The Picture that is Not in the Colors: Cage, Coomaraswamy, and the Impact of India', in *John Cage: Music, Philosophy, and Intention, 1933–1950*, ed. David W. Patterson (New York, 2002), pp. 177–215.

3 The account of Cage's experiences at Black Mountain draws principally on David W. Patterson, 'Appraising the Catchwords *c*. 1942–1959: John Cage's Asian-Derived Rhetoric and the Historical Reference of Black Mountain College', PhD dissertation, Columbia University, 1996, pp. 190–234.

4 In Richard Kostelanetz, ed., *John Cage: An Anthology* (New York, 1991), pp. 77–84.

5 Jean-Jacques Nattiez and Robert Samuels, eds, *The Boulez-Cage Correspondence* (Cambridge, 1993), p. 46.

6 B. H. Friedman, ed., *Give My Regards to Eighth Street: Collected Writings of Morton Feldman* (Cambridge, MA, 2000), p. 5.

7 Alan Watts, *Zen* (Stanford, CA, 1948) – the volume was an expanded edition of *Zen Buddhism: A New Outline and Introduction* (London, 1947); *The Huang Po Doctrine of Universal Mind*, trans. Chu Ch'an [John Blofeld] (London, 1947). See the discussion of *The Huang Po Doctrine* below.

8 Watts, *Zen*, p. 39; John Cage, 'Lecture on Nothing', in *Silence: Lectures and Writings* (Middletown, CT, 1961), p. 113.

9 Nattiez and Samuels, eds, *The Boulez-Cage Correspondence*, p. 50.

10 David W. Patterson, 'Cage and Asia: History and Sources', in *The Cambridge Companion to John Cage*, ed. David Nicholls (Cambridge, 2002), p. 53.

11 Richard Kostelanetz, ed., *Conversing with Cage*, 2nd edn (New York, 2002), pp. 54–5.

12 John Cage, 'Composition as Process, III: Communication', in *Silence*, pp. 46–7.

13 *The Huang Po Doctrine of Universal Mind*, p. 24.

14 John Cage and Daniel Charles, *For the Birds: John Cage in Conversation with Daniel Charles*, ed. Tom Gora and John Cage, trans. Richard Gardner (Boston, 1981), p. 43.

15 John Cage, 'Composition as Process, II: Indeterminacy', in *Silence*, p. 36.

16 Nattiez and Samuels, eds, *The Boulez-Cage Correspondence*, p. 112.

17 Cage, *Silence*, pp. 109 and 119.

18 Ibid., p. 131.

19 David Revill, *The Roaring Silence: John Cage, A Life* (New York, 1992), p. 166.

20 Reprinted in Pierre Boulez, *Stocktakings from an Apprenticeship*, trans. Stephen Walsh (Oxford, 1991), pp. 26–38; J. B., 'Look, No Hands! And It's "Music"', *New York Times*, 15 April 1954, p. 34.

21 See the entertaining account in Kenneth Silverman, *Begin Again: A Biography of John Cage* (New York, 2010), 146–8.

22 Ross Parmenter, 'Music: Experimenter; Zounds! Sounds by John Cage at Town Hall', *New York Times*, 16 May 1958, p. 20.

23 John Cage, *A Year from Monday: New Lectures and Writings* (Middletown, CT, 1967), p. 136.

24 Cage, 'Composition as Process, III', in *Silence*, p. 49. For more, see also Christopher Shultis, 'Cage and Europe', in *The Cambridge Companion to John Cage*, ed. Nicholls, pp. 31–40.

4 Eminence

1 See Jennifer DeLapp-Birkett, 'Aaron Copland and the Politics of Twelve-Tone Composition in the Early Cold War United States', *Journal of Musicological Research*, XXVII/1 (2008), pp. 31–62.

2 John Cage, *Silence: Lectures and Writings* (Middletown, CT, 1961), pp. 261–2.

3 Cage, *Silence*, p. 275.

4 Reprinted in Richard Kostelanetz, ed., *John Cage: An Anthology* (New York, 1991), pp. 153–7.

5 Jean-Jacques Nattiez and Robert Samuels, eds, *The Boulez-Cage Correspondence* (Cambridge, 1993), p. 48. For 'Who Cares if You Listen', see *The Collected Essays of Milton Babbitt*, ed. Stephen Peles et al. (Princeton, NJ, 2003), pp. 48–54.

6 Carolyn Brown, *Chance and Circumstance: Twenty Years with Cage and Cunningham* (New York, 2007), p. 257.

7 Kostelanetz, ed., *John Cage: An Anthology*, pp. 123–4.

8 Branden W. Joseph, 'Chance, Indeterminacy, Multiplicity', in *The Anarchy of Silence: John Cage and Experimental Art* (Barcelona, 2009),

pp. 231–8. Joseph convincingly argues that artists like Kaprow, Hansen and Higgins – all of whom departed from Cage's example in various ways – nevertheless were greatly affected by Cage's ideas.

9 See Kostelanetz, ed., *John Cage: An Anthology*, pp. 151–3.

10 John Cage, *M: Writings, '67–'72* (Middletown, CT, 1973), p. 137.

11 See Thomas F. Johnson, 'C. F. Peters: Past and Present', *Musical America*, LXXXII/10 (October 1962), pp. 12–13 and Cole Gagne and Tracy Caras, *Soundpieces: Interviews with American Composers* (Metuchen, NJ, 1982), pp. 73–4.

12 Brown, *Chance and Circumstance*, pp. 263–6.

13 Cage, *Silence*, p. 95.

14 Ibid., p. 42.

15 Jill Johnston, 'There is No Silence Now', reprinted in *John Cage: An Anthology*, ed. Richard Kostelanetz, pp. 147–8.

16 John Hollander, '*Silence*', reprinted in *Writings about John Cage*, ed. Richard Kostelanetz (Ann Arbor, MI, 1993), pp. 264–9.

17 See Kostelanetz, ed., *John Cage: An Anthology*, pp. 89–94.

18 Christian Wolff, letter to Gavin Bryars, dated 10 September 1974, quoted in Bryars, 'Vexations and its Performers', *JEMS: An Online Journal of Experimental Music Studies*, (1983); reprinted online 2004, at www.users.waitrose.com/~chobbs/Bryars.html#_ednref6, para. 10 (accessed 18 June 2009).

19 The following narrative regarding Cunningham draws on the account in Brown, *Chance and Circumstance*.

20 James Klosty, ed., *Merce Cunningham* (New York, 1975), p. 55.

21 Brown, *Chance and Circumstance*, pp. 308–9.

22 Ibid., p. 407.

23 Gagne and Caras, *Soundpieces*, p. 75.

24 Alvin Lucier, *Notes in the Margins* (Middletown, CT, 1988), p. 15. I am very grateful to Mr Lucier for giving me a copy of this fascinating, hard-to-find reminiscence.

25 For more documentation of the *Variations V* performances and the personnel involved, see Leta E. Miller, 'Cage, Cunningham, and Collaborators: The Odyssey of *Variations V*', *Musical Quarterly*, LXXXV/3 (2001), pp. 547–67.

26 For more, see Stephen Husarik, 'John Cage and Lejaren Hiller: HPSCHD, 1969', *American Music*, I/2 (Summer 1983), pp. 1–21.

27   See Sara Heimbecker, '*HPSCHD*, Gesamtkunstwerk, and Utopia',
     American Music, XXVI/4 (2008), 474–98.

5 Doyen

1   Richard Kostelanetz, ed., *Conversing with Cage*, 2nd edn (New York,
    2002), pp. 11 and 25.
2   For a description of the work and its performance, see Lowell Cross,
    '*Reunion*: John Cage, Marcel Duchamp, Electronic Music and Chess',
    Leonardo Music Journal, 9 (1999), pp. 35–42.
3   John Cage, *M: Writings, '67–'72* (Middletown, CT, 1973), p. 5.
4   Ibid., p. xv.
5   John Cage and Daniel Charles, *For the Birds: John Cage in Conversation
    with Daniel Charles*, ed. Tom Gora and John Cage, trans. Richard
    Gardner (Boston, 1981), pp. 61–2; David Nicholls, *John Cage* (Urbana,
    IL, 2007), pp. 86–8.
6   John Cage, *Empty Words: Writings, '73–'78* (Middletown, CT, 1979),
    p. 185.
7   James J. Martin, *Men Against the State: The Expositors of Individualist
    Anarchism in America, 1827–1908* (De Kalb, IL, 1953). (Martin was one
    of Cage's neighbours at Stony Point.) For Cage's admiring remarks on
    Martin and Goldman, see Richard Fleming and William Duckworth,
    eds, *John Cage at Seventy-Five* (Lewisburg, PA, 1989), pp. 122–3.
8   Peter Kropotkin, '"Anarchism", from *The Encyclopædia Britannica*',
    in *The Conquest of Bread and Other Writings*, ed. Marshall Shatz
    (Cambridge, 1995), p. 233; Cage and Charles, *For the Birds*, p. 112.
9   Cage, *M*, p. 18.
10 Ibid., p. 70.
11 For a comprehensive study of Cage and Thoreau in the context of
    traditions in American literature and music, see Christopher Shultis,
    *Silencing the Sounded Self: John Cage and the American Experimental
    Tradition* (Boston, 1998).
12 Calvin Tomkins, *The Bride and the Bachelors: The Heretical Courtship
    in Modern Art* (New York, 1965), p. 139.
13 Cage and Charles, *For the Birds*, p. 59.
14 John Cage, 'An Autobiographical Statement', in *John Cage, Writer:*

Previously Uncollected Pieces, ed. Richard Kostelanetz (New York, 1993), p. 113.

15 Laura Fletcher and Thomas Moore, 'John Cage: An Interview', *Sonus*, XIII/2 (Spring 1983), p. 19.

16 Cage, *Empty Words*, pp. 4–5.

17 Cole Gagne and Tracy Caras, *Soundpieces: Interviews with American Composers* (Metuchen, NJ, 1982), pp. 76–7.

18 Kostelanetz, ed., *Conversing with Cage*, p. 146.

19 Cage, *Empty Words*, p. 12.

20 Ibid., p. 75. See Christopher Shultis's sensitive and insightful discussion of *Empty Words* in *Silencing the Sounded Self*, pp. 118–26.

21 Anne Waldman and Marilyn Webb, eds, *Talking Poetics from Naropa Institute: Annals of the Jack Kerouac School of Disembodied Poetics* (Boulder, CO, 1978), vol. 1, p. 219.

22 Ibid., vol. I, p. 217.

23 Ibid., vol. I, pp. 218 and 220.

24 The performance was recorded but not released until 1990; it is currently available (Ampersand Ampere6, 2004). See Kostelanetz, ed., *Conversing with Cage*, pp. 132–3, for Cage's recollection of the event.

25 Cage, *M*, p. xiv.

26 The work is often performed with *Renga* (1976), a piece in which drawings are translated by musicians into graceful musical curves that slide through the frequency range. I discuss Cage's later appropriations of renga poetry in chapter Six.

27 Allen Hughes, 'Hundreds Walk Out of Premiere of John Cage', *New York Times*, 5 November 1976, p. 48.

28 Peter Gena, 'Re: John Cage and Song Books in Buffalo', online posting, 5 December 1997, *Silence: The John Cage Discussion List*, at http://replay.waybackmachine.org/20021019110839andwww.newalbion.com/artists/cagej/silence/html/1997q4/0292.html (accessed 26 March 2011). Thanks to Joseph Zitt for relocating the online reference. Mary Jane Leach, who is co-editing (with Renee Levine Packer) a forthcoming volume of essays about Eastman, has pointed out that he did not have a sister and that there are likely countless conflicting recollections of this celebrated incident (email to Rob Haskins, 25 March 2011).

29 Cage, *Empty Words*, p. 79.

30 Gagne and Caras, *Soundpieces*, p. 71.

31 John Cage, *Musicage: Cage Muses on Words, Art, Music; John Cage in Conversation with Joan Retallack* (Hanover, NH, 1996), pp. 136–7.

32 John Cage, *Etchings, 1978–1982* (Oakland, CA, 1982), p. 38.

33 See Cage, *Etchings*, p. 36, for his own description of the process.

34 Cage, *Musicage*, p. 251.

35 Kathan Brown, *John Cage Visual Art: To Sober and Quiet the Mind* (San Francisco, 2000), pp. 68 and 82.

36 Jeff Goldberg, 'John Cage', *Transatlantic Review*, 55/56 (1976), p. 110.

6 Parting

1 John Cage, *Empty Words: Writings, '73–'78* (Middletown, CT, 1979), p. 184; Cole Gagne and Tracy Caras, *Soundpieces: Interviews with American Composers* (Metuchen, NJ, 1982), p. 81.

2 Rebecca Y. Kim suggests that Cage's voice acted as a medium through which he enacted authorial withdrawal; see the final chapter of 'In No Uncertain Musical Terms: The Cultural Politics of John Cage's Indeterminacy', PhD dissertation, Columbia University, 2008.

3 The following discussion draws from his introduction to *Themes & Variations* in John Cage, *Composition in Retrospect* (Cambridge, MA, 1993), pp. 55–71.

4 Ibid., p. 64.

5 Ibid., pp. 66 and 69.

6 John Cage, *x: Writings '79–'82* (Middletown, CT, 1983), p. 163.

7 For video of both events, see Allan Miller, *John Cage: I Have Nothing To Say and I am Saying It* (New York, 1990) and Peter Greenaway, *4merican Composers: John Cage* (London, 1983).

8 Cage, *x*, p. 123.

9 Brian Brandt, conversation with Rob Haskins, 12 March 2002.

10 Cage made realizations of *Ryoanji* for oboe, flute, voice, trombone and contrabass; he was working on one for cello when he died.

11 For more on Cage's use of time brackets, see Benedict Weisser, 'John Cage: "... The Whole World Potentially Would be Sound": Time-Brackets and the Number Pieces, 1981–92', *Perspectives of New Music*, XLI/2 (2003), pp. 176–225, and Rob Haskins, *Anarchic Societies of Sounds: The Number*

Pieces of John Cage (Saarbrücken, 2009), pp. 79–109.

12 See James Pritchett, James Tenney, Andrew Culver and Frances White, 'Cage and the Computer: A Panel Discussion', in *Writings through John Cage's Music, Poetry, and Art*, ed. David W. Bernstein and Christopher Hatch (Chicago, IL, 2001), pp. 193–8.

13 Kathan Brown, *John Cage Visual Art: To Sober and Quiet the Mind* (San Francisco, CA, 2000), pp. 89–97.

14 Ibid., pp. 97–102.

15 John Cage, *New River Watercolors* (Richmond, VA, 1988).

16 Jeremy Millar et al., *Every Day is a Good Day: The Visual Art of John Cage* (London, 2010), pp. 146–51.

17 Wulf Herzogenrath, 'John Cage: An Artist Who Accepts Life', in Wulf Herzogenrath and Andreas Kreul, *Sounds of the Inner Eye: John Cage, Mark Tobey, Morris Graves* (Tacoma, WA, 2002), pp. 17–18.

18 James Pritchett, 'Understanding John Cage's Chance Music: An Analytical Approach', in *John Cage at Seventy-Five*, ed. Richard Fleming and William Duckworth (Lewisburg, PA, 1989), pp. 249–61.

19 James Pritchett, *The Music of John Cage* (Cambridge, 1993); Christopher Shultis, *Sounding the Silenced Self: John Cage and the American Experimental Tradition* (Boston, MA, 1998); Brown, *John Cage Visual Art*.

20 John Cage, 'Anarchy', in *John Cage at Seventy-Five*, p. 194.

21 'About the Kyoto Prize', at www.inamori-f.or.jp/e_kp_out_out.html (accessed 1 April 2011).

22 Pauline Oliveros, 'Mission Statement', at the Deep Listening Institute, http://deeplistening.org/site/content/about (accessed 1 April 2011).

23 Haskins, *Anarchic Societies of Sounds*, pp. 127–8.

24 *Two²* does not employ time brackets.

25 For more on Cage's thoughts on this aspect of Duchamp's work, see John Cage, *Musicage: Cage Muses on Words, Art, Music; John Cage in Conversation with Joan Retallack* (Hanover, NH, 1996), pp. 103–5.

26 For a description of the compositional process of *Two²*, see Rob Haskins, 'On John Cage's Late Music, Analysis, and the Model of Renga in *Two²*', *American Music*, XXVII/3 (2009), pp. 327–55.

27 Cage, *Musicage*.

28 Ibid., pp. 169–75.

29 For more, see Christopher Shultis, 'A Living Oxymoron: Norman O. Brown's Criticism of John Cage', *Perspectives of New Music*, XLIV/2

(2006), pp. 66–87.

30 Quoted in Cage, *Musicage*, p. xlii.
31 Cage, *Musicage*, p. 228.
32 David Revill, *The Roaring Silence: John Cage, a Life* (New York, 1992), p. 302.

Epilogue

1 John Rockwell, *All American Music: Composition in the Late Twentieth Century* (New York, 1983), p. 53.
2 See www.john-cage.halberstadt.de/new/index.php?seite=chronik&l=e and 'One Thousand Hear Change of Note in World's Longest Concert', at www.dw-world.de/dw/article/0,,3463502,00.html (accessed 13 April 2010).
3 James Pritchett, 'The Completion of John Cage's *Freeman Etudes*', *Perspectives of New Music*, XXXII/2 (Summer 1994), pp. 264–71.
4 Richard Taruskin, *The Oxford History of Western Music* (Oxford, 2005), vol. V, pp. 63–5. For that matter, similarly inclined avant-garde composers, including Pierre Boulez, Milton Babbitt and others, adopted a much more nuanced approach to the technical and aesthetic underpinnings of their work soon after completing their earliest compositions. See Joseph Straus, *Twelve-Tone Composition in America* (Cambridge, 2010) for a good introduction.
5 Taruskin, *Oxford History of Western Music*, vol. V, p. 71.
6 John Cage, *Silence: Lectures and Writings* (Middletown, CT, 1961), p. 36.
7 Taruskin, *Oxford History of Western Music*, vol. V, p. 76. The Tan quotation was first published in David Revill, *The Roaring Silence: John Cage, A Life* (New York, 1992), p. 190.
8 Margaret Leng Tan, email to Rob Haskins, 29 March 2011. See also Tan, 'John Cage Poses a Few Last Questions', *New York Times*, 1 August 1993, p. 2.27, which describes her last meeting with Cage the day before his fatal stroke.

Bibliography

Archival Sources

Cage's musical manuscripts and sketches are held at the New York Public Library; correspondence (including letters to various composers connected with the project published as *Notations* [1969]) is archived at Northwestern University, Evanston, Illinois; Wesleyan University (Middleton, Connecticut) holds sources related to Cage's literary works; and the collection of Cage's books on mycology is held by the University of California Santa Cruz.

Writings by John Cage

This chronological list does not include separate entries for specific Cage essays cited in the text because all of those writings are published in books listed in this bibliography; see the references to locate those sources.

Silence: Lectures and Writings (Middletown, CT, 1961)
A Year from Monday: New Lectures and Writings (Middletown, CT, 1967)
Notations (New York, 1969)
M: Writings, '67–'72 (Middletown, CT, 1973)
For the Birds: John Cage in Conversation with Daniel Charles, ed. Tom Gora and John Cage, trans. Richard Gardner (Boston, MA, 1981)
Themes & Variations (Barrytown, NY, 1982)
X: Writings, '79–'82 (Middletown, CT, 1983)
'MUSHROOMS et Variationes', in *The Guests Go in to Supper*, ed. Melody Sumner, Kathleen Burch and Michael Sumner (Santa Fe, NM, 1986),

pp. 28–96

*I–VI: MethodStructureIntentionDisciplineNotationIndeterminacyInterpenetra-
    tionImitationDevotionCircumstancesVariableStructureNonunderstanding-
    ContingencyInconsistencyPerformance* (Cambridge, MA, 1990)

John Cage, Writer: Previously Uncollected Pieces, ed. Richard Kostelanetz
    (New York, 1993)

Composition in Retrospect (Cambridge, MA, 1993)

'Overpopulation and Art', in *John Cage: Composed in America*, ed. Marjorie
    Perloff and Charles Junkerman (Chicago, IL, 1994), pp. 14–38

'Mesostics', in *Ästhetik und Komposition: zur Aktualität der Darmstädter
    Ferienkursarbeit*, ed. Gianmario Borio and Ulrich Mosch (Mainz, 1994),
    pp. 7–11

*Musicage: Cage Muses on Words, Art, Music; John Cage in Conversation with
    Joan Retallack* (Hanover, NH, 1996)

Anarchy (Middletown, CT, 2001)

Exhibition Catalogues

Addiss, Stephen, and Ray Kass, eds, *John Cage: Zen Ox-Herding Pictures* (New
    York, 2009)

The Anarchy of Silence: John Cage and Experimental Art (Barcelona, 2009)

Cage, John, *Arbeiten auf Papier* (Wiesbaden, 1992)

—, *Etchings, 1978–1982* (Oakland, CA, 1982)

—, *New River Watercolors* (Richmond, VA, 1988)

Herzogenrath, Wulf, and Andreas Kreul, *Sounds of the Inner Eye: John Cage,
    Mark Tobey, Morris Graves* (Tacoma, WA, 2002)

Kass, Ray, *The Sight of Silence: John Cage's Complete Watercolors* (Roanoke,
    VA, 2011)

Millar, Jeremy, et al., *Every Day is a Good Day: The Visual Art of John Cage*
    (London, 2010)

Rolywholyover: A Circus (New York, 1993)

Other Sources

'About the Kyoto Prize', http://www.inamori-f.or.jp/e_kp_out_out.html (accessed 1 April 2011)

Artaud, Antonin, *The Theater and its Double*, trans. Mary Caroline Richards (New York, 1958)

B., J., 'Look, No Hands! And It's "Music"', *New York Times*, 15 April 1954, p. 34

Baynes, Cary F., trans., *The I Ching, or Book of Changes: The Richard Wilhelm Translation Rendered into English* (Princeton, NJ, 1950)

Bernstein, David W., 'Music, I: To the late 1940s,' in *The Cambridge Companion to John Cage*, ed. David Nicholls (Cambridge, MA, 2002), pp. 63–84

—, and Christopher Hatch, eds, *Writings through John Cage's Music, Poetry, and Art* (Chicago, IL, 2001)

Blofeld, John, trans., *The Zen Teaching of Huang Po on the Transmission of Mind* (New York, 1994)

Boulez, Pierre, *Stocktakings from an Apprenticeship*, trans. Stephen Walsh (Oxford, 1991)

Brandt, Brian, conversation with Rob Haskins, 12 March 2002

Brown, Carolyn, *Chance and Circumstance: Twenty Years with Cage and Cunningham* (New York, 2007)

Brown, Kathan, *John Cage Visual Art: To Sober and Quiet the Mind* (San Francisco, CA, 2000)

—, 'Visual Art', in *The Cambridge Companion to John Cage*, ed. David Nicholls (Cambridge, 2002), pp. 109–27

Broyles, Michael, 'Art Music from 1860 to 1920', in *The Cambridge History of American Music*, ed. David Nicholls (Cambridge, 1998), pp. 214–54

Bryars, Gavin, 'Vexations and its Performers', *JEMS: An Online Journal of Experimental Music Studies* (1983), reprinted online 2004, at www.users.waitrose.com/~chobbs/Bryars.html#_ednref6 (accessed 18 June 2009)

Carter, David, 'Surface Noise: A Cageian Approach to Electronica', *Popular Music Online*, 1 (2009), at www.popular-musicology-online.com/issues/01/carter-01.html (accessed 22 March 2011)

The Collected Essays of Milton Babbitt, ed. Stephen Peles et al. (Princeton, NJ, 2003)

'Composer Pays for Piece of Silence', CNN [online], http://articles.cnn.com/2002-09-23/entertainment/uk.silence_1_peters-edition-nicholas-riddle-john-cage-trust?_s=pm:showbiz (accessed 26 May 2011)

Cowell, Henry, *New Musical Resources*, ed. David Nicholls (Cambridge, 1995)

—, 'Who is the Greatest Living Composer?', *Northwest Musical Herald*, 7 (March–April 1933), p. 7

—, ed., *American Composers on American Music* (Stanford, CA, 1933)

Cross, Lowell, '*Reunion*: John Cage, Marcel Duchamp, Electronic Music and Chess', *Leonardo Music Journal*, 9 (1999), pp. 35–42

DeLapp-Birkett, Jennifer, 'Aaron Copland and the Politics of Twelve-Tone Composition in the Early Cold War United States', *Journal of Musicological Research*, XXVII/1 (2008), pp. 31–62

Fleming, Richard, and William Duckworth, eds, *John Cage at Seventy-Five* (Lewisburg, PA, 1989)

Fletcher, Laura, and Thomas Moore, 'John Cage: An Interview', *Sonus*, XIII/2 (Spring 1983), pp. 16–23

Friedman, B. H., *Give My Regards to Eighth Street: Collected Writings of Morton Feldman* (Cambridge, MA, 2000)

Gagne, Cole, and Tracy Caras, *Soundpieces: Interviews with American Composers* (Metuchen, NJ, 1982)

Gann, Kyle, *No Such Thing as Silence: John Cage's '4'33"'* (New Haven, CT, 2009)

Gena, Peter, 'Re: John Cage and Song Books in Buffalo', online posting, 5 December 1997, *Silence: The John Cage Discussion List*, http://replay. waybackmachine.org/20021019110839/http://www.newalbion.com/ artists/cagej/silence/html/1997q4/0292.html (accessed 26 March 2011)

Goldberg, Jeff, 'John Cage', *Transatlantic Review*, 55/56 (1976), pp. 103–10

Greenaway, Peter, *4merican Composers: John Cage* [video] (London, 1983)

Gropius, Walter, et al., *The Theater of the Bauhaus*, trans. Arthur S. Wensinger (Middletown, CT, 1961)

Haskins, Rob, *Anarchic Societies of Sounds: The Number Pieces of John Cage* (Saarbrücken, 2009)

—, 'John Cage and Recorded Sound: A Discographical Essay', *Notes: The Journal of the Music Library Association*, LXVII/2 (2010), pp. 382–409

—, 'On John Cage's Late Music, Analysis, and the Model of Renga in *Two²*', *American Music*, XXVII/3 (2009), pp. 327–55

Heimbecker, Sara, '*HPSCHD*, Gesamtkunstwerk, and Utopia', *American Music*, XXVI/4 (2008), pp. 474–98

Herwitz, Daniel, *Making Theory/Constructing Art: On the Authority of the Avant-Garde* (Chicago, IL, 1993)

Herzogenrath, Wulf, 'John Cage: An Artist Who Accepts Life', in Wulf
    Herzogenrath and Andreas Kreul, *Sounds of the Inner Eye: John Cage,
    Mark Tobey, Morris Graves* (Tacoma, WA, 2002), pp. 2–23
Hicks, Michael, 'Cage's Studies with Schoenberg', *American Music*, VIII/2
    (1990), pp. 125–40
—, *Henry Cowell, Bohemian* (Urbana, IL, 2002)
Hines, Thomas J., '"Then Not Yet 'Cage'": The Los Angeles Years,
    1912–1938', in *John Cage: Composed in America*, ed. Marjorie Perloff and
    Charles Junkerman (Chicago, IL, 1994), pp. 65–99
Hollander, John, '*Silence*', reprinted in *Writings about John Cage*, ed. Richard
    Kostelanetz (Ann Arbor, MI, 1993), pp. 264–9
The Huang Po Doctrine of Universal Mind, trans. Chu Ch'an [John Blofeld]
    (London, 1947)
Hughes, Allen, 'Hundreds Walk Out of Premiere of John Cage', *New York
    Times*, 5 November 1976, p. 48
Husarik, Stephen, 'John Cage and Lejaren Hiller: HPSCHD, 1969', *American
    Music*, I/2 (Summer 1983), pp. 1–21
Johnson, Thomas F., 'C. F. Peters: Past and Present', *Musical America*,
    LXXXII/10 (October 1962), pp. 12–13
Johnston, Jill, 'There is No Silence Now', in *John Cage: An Anthology*, ed.
    Richard Kostelanetz (New York, 1994), pp. 145–9
Joseph, Branden W., 'Chance, Indeterminacy, Multiplicity', in *The Anarchy
    of Silence: John Cage and Experimental Art* (Barcelona, 2009), pp. 210–38
Kim, Rebecca Y., 'In No Uncertain Musical Terms: The Cultural Politics of
    John Cage's Indeterminacy', PhD dissertation, Columbia University,
    2008
Klosty, James, *Merce Cunningham* (New York, 1975)
Kostelanetz, Richard, ed., *Conversing with Cage*, 2nd edn (New York, 2002)
—, ed., *John Cage: An Anthology* (New York, 1994)
—, ed., *Writings about John Cage* (Ann Arbor, MI, 1993)
Kropotkin, Peter, '"Anarchism", from *The Encyclopædia Britannica*', in *The
    Conquest of Bread and Other Writings*, ed. Marshall Shatz (Cambridge,
    1995), pp. 233–47
Leach, Mary Jane, email to Rob Haskins, 25 March 2011
Levitz, Tamara, 'Syvilla Fort's African Modernism and John Cage's Gestic
    Music: The Story of *Bacchanale*', *South Atlantic Quarterly*, CIV/1 (2005),
    pp. 123–49

Lucier, Alvin, *Notes in the Margins* (Middletown, CT, 1988)

Martin, James J., *Men Against the State: The Expositors of Individualist Anarchism in America, 1827–1908* (De Kalb, IL, 1953)

Mary, Maureen, 'Letters: The Brief Love of John Cage for Pauline Schindler, 1934–1935', *ex tempore*, VIII/1 (1996), pp. 1–26

Mattis, Olivia, 'Conversation with John Cage, New York City (in Cage's Apartment), 28 July 1988, 4–5:15 p.m.' (unpublished)

Miller, Allan, *John Cage: I Have Nothing to Say and I am Saying It* [video] (New York, 1990)

Miller, Leta E., 'Cage, Cunningham, and Collaborators: The Odyssey of *Variations V*', *Musical Quarterly*, LXXXV/3 (2001), pp. 547–67

—, 'Cultural Intersections: John Cage in Seattle, 1938–1940', in *John Cage: Music, Philosophy, and Intention, 1933–1950*, ed. David W. Patterson (New York, 2002), pp. 47–82

—, 'Henry Cowell and John Cage: Intersections and Influences, 1933–1945', *Journal of the American Musicological Society*, LIX/1 (2006), pp. 47–112

Nattiez, Jean-Jacques, and Robert Samuels, eds, *The Boulez-Cage Correspondence* (Cambridge, 1993)

Nicholls, David, 'Cowell, Henry', in *Grove Music Online. Oxford Music Online*, at www.oxfordmusiconline.com/subscriber/article/grove/music/06743 (accessed 16 March 2011)

—, *John Cage* (Urbana, IL, 2007)

—, ed., *The Cambridge Companion to John Cage* (Cambridge, 2002)

Oliveros, Pauline, 'Mission Statement', at the Deep Listening Institute, http://deeplistening.org/site/content/about (accessed 1 April 2011)

Patterson, David W., 'Appraising the Catchwords, *c*. 1942–1959: John Cage's Asian-Derived Rhetoric and the Historical Reference of Black Mountain College', PhD dissertation, Columbia University, 1996

—, 'Cage and Asia: History and Sources', in *The Cambridge Companion to John Cage*, ed. David Nicholls (Cambridge, 2002), pp. 41–59

—, 'The Picture that is Not in the Colors: Cage, Coomaraswamy, and the Impact of India', in *John Cage: Music, Philosophy, and Intention, 1933–1950*, ed. David W. Patterson (New York, 2002), pp. 177–215

—, ed., *John Cage: Music, Philosophy, and Intention, 1933–1950* (New York, 2002)

Perloff, Marjorie, and Charles Junkerman, eds, *John Cage: Composed in America* (Chicago, IL, 1994)

Pritchett, James, *The Music of John Cage* (Cambridge, 1993)

—, 'Understanding John Cage's Chance Music: An Analytical Approach', in *John Cage at Seventy-Five*, ed. Richard Fleming and William Duckworth (Lewisburg, PA, 1989), pp. 249–61

—, 'What Silence Taught John Cage: The Story of *4'33"*', in *The Anarchy of Silence: John Cage and Experimental Art* (Barcelona, 2009), pp. 166–77

Reidy, Brent, 'Our Memory of What Happened is Not What Happened: Cage, Metaphor, and Myth', *American Music*, XXVIII/2 (2010), pp. 211–27.

Retallack, Joan, *The Poethical Wager* (Berkeley, CA, 2003)

—, James Tenney, Andrew Culver and Frances White, 'Cage and the Computer: A Panel Discussion', in *Writings through John Cage's Music, Poetry, and Art*, ed. David W. Bernstein and Christopher Hatch (Chicago, IL, 2001), pp. 190–209

Revill, David, *The Roaring Silence: John Cage, a Life* (New York, 1992)

Rockwell, John, *All American Music: Composition in the Late Twentieth Century* (New York, 1983)

Schwartz, Stephen, *From West to East: California and the Making of the American Mind* (New York, 1998)

Shultis, Christopher, 'Cage and Europe', in *The Cambridge Companion to John Cage*, ed. David Nicholls (Cambridge, 2002), pp. 20–40

—, 'A Living Oxymoron: Norman O. Brown's Criticism of John Cage', *Perspectives of New Music*, XLIV/2 (2006), pp. 67–87

—, *Silencing the Sounded Self: John Cage and the American Experimental Tradition* (Boston, MA, 1998)

Silverman, Kenneth, *Begin Again: A Biography of John Cage* (New York, 2010)

Straus, Joseph N., *Twelve-Tone Music in America* (Cambridge, 2009)

Tan, Margaret Leng, email to Rob Haskins, 29 March 2011

—, 'John Cage Poses a Few Last Questions', *New York Times*, 1 August 1993, p. 2.27

Taruskin, Richard, *The Danger of Music and Other Anti-Utopian Essays* (Berkeley, CA, 2010)

—, *The Oxford History of Western Music*, 6 vols (Oxford, 2005)

Thomson, Virgil, 'Expressive Percussion', in *John Cage: An Anthology*, ed. Richard Kostelanetz (New York, 1994), pp. 71–3

Thorman, Marc, 'Speech and Text in Compositions by John Cage, 1950–1992', DMA dissertation, City University of New York, 2002

—, 'John Cage's Letters to Erik Satie', *American Music*, XXIV/1 (2006), pp. 95–123

Tomkins, Calvin, *The Bride and the Bachelors: The Heretical Courtship in Modern Art* (New York, 1965)

Waldman, Anne, and Marilyn Webb, eds, *Talking Poetics from Naropa Institute: Annals of the Jack Kerouac School of Disembodied Poetics*, 2 vols (Boulder, CO, 1978)

Watts, Alan, *Zen* (Stanford, CA, 1948)

Weisser, Benedict, 'John Cage: ". . . The Whole World Potentially Would be Sound": Time-Brackets and the Number Pieces, 1981–92', *Perspectives of New Music*, XLI/2 (2003), pp. 176–225

Internet

Chaudon, André, *John Cage Database*
www.johncage.info

Emmerik, Paul van, Herbert Henck and András Wilheim, *A John Cage Compendium*
www.xs4all.nl/~cagecomp

The John Cage Trust
http://johncage.org

Pritchett, James, *Writings on John Cage (and Others)*
www.rosewhitemusic.com/cage/index.html

Ronsen, Josh, *John Cage Online*
http://ronsen.org/cagelinks.html

Silence: The John Cage Discussion List
https://lists.virginia.edu/sympa/info/silence

UbuWeb ['a completely independent resource dedicated to all strains of the avant-garde, ethnopoetics, and outsider arts']
www.ubu.com

Select Discography

Cage made more than 300 compositions; with the exception of the 25-Year Retrospective Concert, items in this list appear in chronological order of composition and by the title of the composition in question, not the title of the recording.

Sonata for Clarinet (1933), John Anderson (Etcetera KTC 3002, 1992)

Imaginary Landscape No. 1 (1939), Percussion Group Cincinnati (Mode 229, 2011)

First Construction (in Metal) (1939), Amadinda Percussion Group and Zoltán Kocsis (Hungaroton HCD 31844, 1999)

Bacchanale (1940), Margaret Leng Tan (New Albion NA070, 1994)

Credo in US (1942), Quatuor Hêlios (Wergo WER 6651, 2001)

Four Walls (1944), Margaret Leng Tan and Joan La Barbara (New Albion NA037CD, 1991)

Sonatas and Interludes for Prepared Piano (1946–48), Philipp Vandré (Mode 50, 1996)

The Seasons (1947), American Composers Orchestra and Dennis Russell Davies (ECM 1696, 2000)

String Quartet in Four Parts (1950), LaSalle Quartet (Brilliant Classics 9187, 2010)

Concerto for Prepared Piano and Chamber Orchestra (1950–51), Margaret Leng Tan, American Composers Orchestra and Dennis Russell Davies (ECM 1696, 2000)

The 25-Year Retrospective Concert of the Music of John Cage, John Cage et al. (Wergo 6247-2, 1994)

Indeterminacy (1958), John Cage and David Tudor (Smithsonian/Folkways SF 40804/05, 1992)

Aria (1958), Cathy Berberian (Time Records Series 2000 S/8003, 1961 or 1962)

Cartridge Music (1960), David Tudor, Takehisa Kosugi and Michael Pugliese
(Mode 24, 1991)

Atlas Eclipticalis with *Winter Music* (1961–2), David Tudor, S.E.M. Ensemble
and Petr Kotik (Asphodel 2000, 2000)

Variations III (1963), Motion Ensemble (Mode 129, 2003)

Variations IV (1963), John Cage and David Tudor (Legacy 439, 2000)

Diary: How to Improve the World (You Can Only Make Matters Worse) (1967–
82), John Cage (Wergo 6231-2, 1992)

HPSCHD (1969), Robert Conant and Joel Chadabe (Electronic Music
Foundation EMF CD 038, 2003)

Cheap Imitation (1969), John Cage (Cramps CRS CD 117, 1989)

'Solo for Voice 58' from *Song Books* (1970), Amelia Cuni, Werner Durand,
Raymond Kaczynski and Federico Sanesi (Other Minds OM 1010-2, 2007)

Empty Words, part 3 (1973–4), John Cage (Ampersand Ampere6, 2004)

Etudes Australes (1974), Grete Sultan (Wergo 6152-2, 1987)

Freeman Etudes, Books One and Two (1977–80), Irvine Arditti (Mode 32, 1993)

Hymns and Variations (1979), Vocal Group Ars Nova (Mode 71, 1998)

Roaratorio (1979), John Cage, Joe Heaney, Seamus Ennis, Paddy Glackin,
Matt Malloy, Peadher Mercier and Mell Mercier (Mode 28/29, 2002)

Mirakus² (1984), Joan La Barbara (New Albion Records NA 035, 1990)

Ryoanji (version for bass, 1984), Stefano Scodanibbio (Wergo 6713-2, 2009)

Sculptures Musicales (1989), Chance Operations Collective of Kalamazoo
(OgreOgress 634479962141, 2008)

Two² (1989), Rob Haskins and Laurel Karlik Sheehan (Mode 193, 2008)

Europeras 3 & 4 (1990), Long Beach Opera (Mode 38/39, 1995)

Fourteen (1990), Stephen Drury and the Callithumpian Consort of New
England Conservatory (Mode 57, 1997)

Freeman Etudes, Books Three and Four (1980; 1989–90), Irvine Arditti
(Mode 37, 1994)

Four³ (1991), Martine Joste, Ami Flammer, Dominique Alchourroun and
Jean Michaut (Mode 44, 1995)

One¹⁰ (1992), Irvine Arditti (Mode 100, 2001)

Seventy-four (1992), American Composers Orchestra and Dennis Russell
Davies (ECM 1696, 2000)

Four⁶ (1992), John Cage, Joan La Barbara, Leonard Stein and William
Winant (Music and Arts CD-875, 1995)

Thirteen (1992), Ensemble 13 and Manfred Reichert (CPO 999 227-2, 1993)

Acknowledgements

I am grateful to so many individuals that a comprehensive list would not only be difficult to read, but would inevitably be woefully incomplete. I do, however, want to thank a small subset of the whole: Vivian Constantinopoulos, editorial director at Reaktion Books, for her patience and grace; Laura Kuhn, the director of the John Cage Trust, for her good humour and boundless support; Joan Retallack, who recommended me for this project and whose writing has significantly shaped my own thoughts on Cage; Brian Brandt of Mode Records, for making available so many wonderful recordings of Cage's music – so many, in fact, that I still find myself discovering music of his that I hadn't heard before; Margaret Leng Tan, for her wonderful performances; George Adams, for inspiration and valuable research assistance; many friends who read parts of the manuscript – in particular Ira Byelick, R. A. Moulds and Scott Pender; the University of New Hampshire College of Liberal Arts, for funding of my work; and students and colleagues who make my work both rewarding and entertaining.

For more indispensable support, I thank my parents and my two cats, Harley and Freia. And for her great friendship and the many rich musical experiences that I've shared with her for almost 30 years, I thank, last and most of all, Laurel Karlik Sheehan.

Photo Acknowledgements

The author and the publishers wish to express their thanks to the below sources of illustrative material and/or permission to reproduce it:

Used by permission of the John Cage Trust: pp. 6, 11, 16, 17, 19, 26, 49, 55, 56, 81, 97 (Herve Glogauen), 102, 123, 124, 135, 138, 145 (Rene Block); used by permission of the Cunningham Dance Foundation/Merce Cunningham Trust: p. 90; used by permission of the Electronic Music Foundation: p. 99; © 1960, Henmar Press, used by permission of C. F. Peters Corporation: pp. 70, 79; © 1975, Henmar Press, used by permission of C. F. Peters Corporation: p. 112; © 1984, Henmar Press, used by permission of C. F. Peters Corporation: p. 132; used by permission of George Hirose: p. 153; used by permission of James Klosty: pp. 75, 106; Giovanni Pancino: p. 108; used courtesy of the Rose Art Museum, Brandeis University, Waltham, Massachusetts: p. 95; used by permission of Friends of the Schindler House, Schindler Family Collection: p. 33; © Arnold Schönberg Center Wien. Used by permission of the Arnold Schönberg Center Wien: p. 36 (Florence Homolka).

Reprinted by permission of the publisher from *I-VI* by John Cage, p. 258, Cambridge, Mass.: Harvard University Press, © 1990 by the President and Fellows of Harvard College: p. 10.